Good Morning!
Isn't It a Fabulous Day!

Good Morning!
Isn't It a Fabulous Day!

Parables for Wives and Mothers

by
Nancy Hoag

Beacon Hill Press of Kansas City
Kansas City, Missouri

Cover: Royce Ratcliff

10   9   8   7   6   5   4   3   2

I dedicate this book to
the memory of Betty Reynolds,
my friend.

Contents

Preface

Saying, "I do," is the easy part. Meaning it day after day, year after year, and with children growing faster than your savings account can, on occasion, seems like just plain hard work. All uphill—or the pits! But on those days when we feel surrounded by enemies (and dirty wash), we have only to turn to the pages of God's Word. We read that if we'll commit everything to Him, He will help us, direct our steps, and give us every blessing and wonderful peace. Right?

Well, yes, that is what God's Word says, and we will see all those good things come to pass—eventually. There are days, however, when I question God's timing. I wonder how it is He and I never seem to be working with our watches synchronized. I wonder why we can't simply skip the chores and get to the dessert. And I work myself into a first-class ferment before I flip to even one prescribed passage of His trustworthy Word.

It's those self-induced disruptions, for the most part, I've decided to tuck into this book. Not for safekeeping but for you. Because Titus 2:4 says we older women (not easy to admit that one: older) are to teach the younger women how to live. Because, in my near-50 years, I've been encouraged and even rescued by other women, women just like you and like me: women dealing with the same ups and downs, teetering on the same growing edge, each trying to be God's woman around the clock but some days botching it.

It is my prayer that these *Parables* will tickle your funny bone, move you to tears, and remind you that God is faithful, that His arm is not shortened, that our times are in His hands, and that He will not allow us (or our children and mates) to be tested beyond what we are able to bear.

All my love in Christ.

> Charm is deceptive,
> and beauty is fleeting;
> but a woman who fears the Lord
> is to be praised.
> *Prov. 31:30, NIV*

PART 1

FOR WIVES

Don't be concerned about the outward beauty
that depends on jewelry,
or beautiful clothes,
or hair arrangement.
Be beautiful inside,
in your hearts,
with the lasting charm of a gentle and quiet spirit
which is so precious to God.
That kind of deep beauty was seen in the saintly
women of old, who trusted God and fitted in
with their husbands' plans.

1 Pet. 3:3-5, TLB

Love, Honor, and Trust Him?

Married just over 24 hours, my bridegroom and I began the first full day of our honeymoon in a sun-drenched, snow-covered, Rocky Mountain lodge.

It was a morning filled with both expectation *and* exasperation. Expectation because, on the downhill side of mid-life, I'd discovered love. Exasperation because I'd married the leader of a National Ski Patrol team—while I knew absolutely nothing about the sport.

A skier for nearly 30 years, my Montanan traversed the slopes more skillfully than most folks cut across dry land. I, on the other hand, couldn't distinguish one ski from another, let alone glide from top of incline to level ground! Furthermore, I'd spent most of my life trusting *no one*. Now, this middle-aged bachelor had danced into my life, drawn me to his long, lean frame, and exclaimed, "Trust *me*."

The agreement (before we married) was that I'd never have to ski.

"But I want to see *you* once in a while," I'd said. "And it's obvious: For five months out of every year, you'll be skiing."

"It won't be that bad," my bachelor said. "But, Babe, it's up to you."

Up to me, I thought. Oh, sure. I'd caught the twinkle in his eye every time he mentioned deep powder snow. Truth was I could either take up tatting or learn how to deal with moguls and spills.

It took several weeks of wrestling, but once I decided, there was no turning back. I'd waited too long for a man like mine. I wasn't about to lose him to a Suzy Chaffee—or fear.

"I'm going to ski," I announced. "And I don't care to discuss it again."

Now, however, as I drew the drapes and faced the mountain, I despaired. Equipped with the best gear (a wedding gift from my groom) and outfitted with the latest ski wear (a gift to myself), I'd been enrolled in a ski school. While my spouse sported with patrollers who defied avalanches and Suicide Gulch, we'd agreed *I'd* stay on the bunny hill. In the beginners' class. With 12 children who were barely 3 feet tall!

13

My husband is a kind man. Patient. So, when I fussed aloud, slammed drawers, and refused breakfast, he wrapped his lanky arms around me and said, "Babe, you'll do great!"

How could I resist such charm? So I scuffled with bulky clothing, shoved my hair up into a scratchy wool hat, and adjusted thick goggles.

Outside our room, where wind-whipped snow bit into my face, I squeezed enormous boots into what seemed more like bear traps than bindings and measured the incline and distance to the ski school chalet.

"I can't do it," I wailed.

"Yes, you can," Scotty said, grinning. "I'll get you down that hill. It's easy. Just trust *me*."

We may be husband and wife, I thought, but he most definitely has a few more things to learn about me!

I squinted toward the lodge's main room, where warm smoke curled above Arizona sandstone. This man's been skiing forever, while I've spent years indoors. Trust him? I don't think I can!

But as if he'd read my thoughts, Scotty hugged me, chuckled good-naturedly, pointed to the class gathering beyond and below our room, and emphasized how short the distance would seem once I'd actually made it down the "slight" slope.

"Oh, all right," I said. "I'll do it."

The plan was to join forces—literally. Scotty explained I'd stand behind him and slip my skis between his. He'd ski, I'd coast. I'd also press my face into his jacket, wrap my arms around his middle, *and* close my eyes.

"Close my *eyes!*" I screeched.

Again he smiled, half-turning to touch my cheek and position my arms at his waist. Then, volunteering one final optimistic pledge, he patted my insulated hands, shouted "Yahoo!" and pushed off.

At first, it wasn't so bad. In fact, I discovered I enjoyed skimming the snow, responsible for nothing, relying completely on someone else.

"This is kind of fun," I mumbled against my partner's broad back.

"What'd I tell you?" Scotty chuckled below his goggles, his words steaming in midair.

I returned the laughter, believing my trailblazer *would* get me safely to the bottom of the snow-crusted descent.

Occasionally we did encounter bumps along the trail. "What was that?" I asked once, trying to sound nonchalant.

14

Scotty threw his head back. I knew he was laughing, but I couldn't hear him for the crackling ice and snow sprays echoing across the hill. Another time, he patted my hands and said something about "not to worry" and "just hang on."

To my surprise and his, I did *exactly* as instructed.

However, nearing the bottom of the grade, we began picking up speed.

Scotty had explained we'd accelerate "a bit." But hearing him tell it and experiencing this sensation suddenly seemed like two diverse events. I knew I'd been given his promise that we wouldn't fail, but my skis were starting to part some. And my old nature was beginning to deal with my newborn faith.

"How much farther!" I uttered in a near-silent shriek. Afraid, now, to make a sound for fear . . .

"We're doing great," my leader assured. "Just relax."

About this time, my husband's word began to mean absolutely nothing at all, however, as *my* fears and *my* evaluation of our chances became all the proof I needed: That we would crash (and break every bone in my body) seemed inevitable. And, though I detected no tension in my mate's down-padded trunk, my own stiffened so completely that I soon became even less flexible than the fiberglass skis supporting my rigid form.

"Relax!" my mate shouted back over his shoulder.

"I can't!" I cried.

"You've got to, Babe! We're nearly there. *Trust* me."

Scotty's assurance was no match for my doubt. Although he tried preventing it, within seconds I'd not only begun to tilt but thrown my spouse off balance as well.

Suddenly, four skis, three poles, one pair of goggles, and two prime-of-life bodies rolled, slipped, slid, and bounced across an unrelenting, ice-covered knoll. Not three feet from our goal, all hopes and temporary pleasures came to an unkind end.

As quickly as a bruised man can, Scotty brushed snow from his glasses, shook ice lumps from my hat, questioned me about broken things, and gathered gloves.

"Babe," he said, inspecting, checking, and brushing me, trying also to keep tears from freezing to my face, "do you know what you did?"

I could only nod, shake, and splutter. Both my body and my pride had suffered, and I was certain I'd had all I could bear until I heard the others: my new husband's old buddies.

"Hey!" one ruddy-complexioned Norseman called as seven patrollers shot across the hill. "This must be the new bride!"

"She learning to ski?" another whooped.

"She sure is." Scotty laughed as he lifted me to an upright slant. And pressing his lips to my wounded ear, he whispered, "Learning to trust too. Right?"

A Wife Gives Thanks

Critically, I watched my husband as he stood inside the main entrance in his red usher's jacket, greeting people, passing out bulletins, welcoming newcomers to our church.

Glancing at him as the service began, I thought, How I wish he wouldn't wear that old tie. And why did he get his hair cut so short?

Just then our pastor called the ushers to the altar. Four came, without my husband. He was fumbling under the seat for the basket that he'd set down while talking to a new family who'd just entered the sanctuary. Hastily, he retrieved the basket, stretched his steps, and caught up with the others.

I watched him with the same impatience I'd felt so often lately, wishing he were different, wishing he enjoyed traveling, wishing he'd learn to swim, wishing he'd been promoted and transferred "back home."

"Honestly," I muttered under my breath, "why doesn't he get with it?"

That's when the unmistakable voice of the Lord commanded, "Read Job 14:3."

"Lord," I replied, "how about if I look it up at home? Our pastor is speaking and getting ready to lead us in prayer."

The command was there again. "Read Job 14:3. *Now.*"

I hurriedly flipped through my Bible, eager to read the passage but also anxious to get back to the teaching for the morning. I soon located the scripture, put my finger under the verse, and read, "Must you be so harsh with frail men, and demand an accounting from them?" (TLB).

Tears filled my eyes. I looked up toward the altar as the pastor began reading the scripture for the day, and I watched my husband amble up the aisle with those long, slow strides of his. Except for my pounding heart, everything in me became still. Although the pastor was just introducing his sermon, the Lord had already tutored a delinquent in need of private instruction.

As my spouse slipped into the pew and hugged my hand, my heart cried out, "Father, forgive my silent sins against my husband. He didn't hear me, but You did. Thank You for helping me see what I was doing.

"And, Father, thank You for my husband. Thank You for the love he shows when, with his lunch pail, he sets out for the bus stop each day, even before the sun has risen. Thank You for the brushing he gives the dog *I* hauled home from the pound. Thank You for the hours he spends at the kitchen table helping our daughter with her math or paying bills for orthodontists, fancy dresses, and puppy shots.

"And thank You for the times he's cared for me while I was so desperately ill. Thank You for the bird feeder he built for me outside our kitchen window. Thank You for all the hours he's spent with me at flea markets, loaded down with all the 'good deals' I've been unable to resist; for the times he's escorted me to plays and baseball games, just because *I* love drama and ballpark hot dogs.

"Thank You for hikes, shared picnics beside a mountain stream, and wanderings in the moonlight to glimpse a herd of elk grazing in the long, summer grass.

"Thank You, Lord, for this unique man, quiet, patient, dependable. Most of all, thank You for letting me see in him a small reflection of the sustaining, unconditional, protective love You have for us. In Jesus' name. Amen."

Sometimes I Don't Feel Hospitable

I don't remember the reason, but I do recall being certain I had one: Blue Monday, bills, or the rainy season? Something. At any rate, when the call came from a friend who wanted to "come right over" with her distraught neighbor, I nearly dissolved. Certain Doris hadn't detected my despair, I responded as cheerily as possible for the mood I nursed.

"Absolutely! Come right over," I insisted. Then I prayed, "Lord, please make me hospitable!"

Several minutes later they arrived. And God did something special, something I couldn't seem to do for myself. He caused me to relax. Tension lifted, and a smile replaced my grimace.

My new friend shared why she'd come, and I began to be glad she had. Tears followed and then prayer.

Watching each woman's summer laughter, as they backed out of our drive, my spirit soared. But the greater bonus came in the next half hour when my phone rang for a second time. Again it was Doris.

"I want to tell you Pam's never, ever felt so warmly welcomed into anyone's home before," she said, adding, "Do you know she cried? Said you made her feel she'd 'come home.' Couldn't believe you'd respond so to a complete stranger."

The experience carried me for months until my hospitality factor was tested again. And, again, I would have failed on my own.

"Honey," my husband asked over dinner one night, "you know we're running a training session at the office. I'm bringing 25 folks in for the week." He paused and I stiffened. "What would you think about my having them all here for dinner one night?"

I gulped, forced calm, thought about "my work" and "my desires," then responded, "Sure, Honey, I'd love it!" Remembering Pinocchio's nose, I touched my own.

For two weeks I wrestled. Yes, I recalled the former episode. In fact, other reminders came to me as well: God had given us our home; it had been dedicated to Him for His use; and both my husband and I were eager for people to come and share what we felt was the Lord's blessing. But this week?

"No," I moaned as the time drew too close, and I tossed myself to sleep.

Finally, one afternoon when I couldn't bear to whimper alone any longer, I called my closest friend for sympathy. Instead I received a scolding.

"Nancy, too few wives these days would say yes. But that's one thing that makes us different. Isn't it?"

"Well, yes," I wailed. "But it's such an awful time; I'm so busy."

"Too busy to bless your husband?"

"So you think I should do it?" I groaned, resignedly, wondering why I hadn't called someone else.

"I think so," she said. "And not just for Scotty, either. You should do it for the others too. Just being in your home will be a treat for them." She paused. "I mean it." Then before I could muster up another excuse, she added, "Wait a minute, and I'll find my lasagna recipe. It's perfect for a crowd."

As I took notes and mentally shopped for cheeses and meats, I gave up. Before I crawled into bed, however, I turned to the Lord and said, "You know I *don't* want to do this. But I want to bless my husband and his friends. So, Father, *please* give me Your nature again. Make me happy to have guests, to give them and my spouse a pleasant evening."

Our company was due at six o'clock on Wednesday, but by Tuesday the Lord had answered my prayer. Again I found myself actually relaxing and looking forward to serving guests. I began preparations that morning, shopped, polished, arranged flowers, baked enough desserts for two trays (I never bake!), and shined every faucet and glass in our home.

At 6 P.M. they arrived. And by evening's end, my husband's happiness and a change in our guests had become obvious.

Every last one of them had come through the door stiff and formal. But as the evening progressed, we began to resemble a family reunion.

The men loosened their ties, helped themselves to seconds, poured my coffee, laughed, and shared. One told me about his new baby. Another was proud of his wife.

"In college and managing at home too," he said, his grin wide.

A younger man who handled cooking detail at his place said my lasagna was even better than his own. And one girl, about the age of my oldest, hung around the kitchen and stirred my motherly instincts.

When the last person said, "Good-bye," with a handshake for Scotty and a hug for me, I praised God and ran to the phone to tell my friend.

"Well, remember," she said, "however we feel about opening up our homes, God is gracious, and He desires that we be the same. We may not always feel hospitable, but we can always turn to Him."

My friend was right. I didn't always do well with company under our roof, but God always did well by me. When folks knocked at our door, I could knock at His. I could count on Him to give me what I needed to entertain strangers and to welcome all guests.

Taxing Patience

Nearly April 15, and my husband hadn't filed the income tax return.

"It should be mailed by now," I badgered. "Well . . . ?"

I waited for an answer, but I received nothing but silence as my spouse continued with some other business he'd mapped out for the day.

Thoroughly exasperated, I rifled papers lying on his desk and realized I could do nothing at all with them without my husband's help.

"I know zero about bookkeeping, finances, or filling out tax forms," I moaned. "But I do know the due date, and from where I sit, I'd say we won't make it!"

By now, however, my husband had moved to the other end of the house, and my wailings fell on no one's ears but my own.

The rest of the morning I worried and scurried around the house at my husband's heels. "Ready, yet? Want me to get a stamp from my purse? Can I run something to the post office for you?" But there was little or no response.

That afternoon I wrestled with my writing assignments and church posters, hoping my high-speed labors would serve as my husband's catalyst. However, that tactic failed too.

Come Saturday, with the deadline now two days off, we discovered our daughter's skylight leaked, the dog had burrowed under the back fence, the car sounded "odd," and the clothesline pole had been blown down overnight. Methodically, my husband began handling each of these tasks.

"Please, can't you let those other things go for a while?" I spluttered.

But as he'd planned both in his head and on his note pad, my spouse phoned a hardware clerk, dragged out a toolbox, and continued with what I saw as sidestepping.

"You'll never get those taxes done," I charged. "I'll just bet they'll still be here a month after they're due!"

Now my husband is a patient man. In fact, I would guess there are few men who'd have tolerated my persistent harangues. But at that point it became obvious: He'd endured my badgering and fidgets *and* had nearly run over me a dozen times, and now he not only had had enough but also had something on his mind to say.

Without fanfare but with his face near mine, he took my hands in his, leaned his shoulders toward me, and in a husky timbre said, "Trust me."

For a moment, I couldn't find my voice. Then I decided it was probably just as well: My husband had said it all.

How many times, I wondered as we stood there in the hallway, had I plagued God just as I'd fussed with my husband? How often had the Lord conveyed a similar message: "Everything is under control. The job is getting done even if you can't see the evidence"?

Hugging my husband, I asked for and received his forgiveness. Then I renewed my vow to trust him for mended clotheslines, corralled dogs, a repaired carburetor, *and* taxes paid on time. And they were.

Amnesty

Last week our library offered to forgive sins. Amnesty Week they named it, and although I'd never heard of such an event, I decided to see if I were one of the guilty who could be excused.

"Nearly two years ago . . . just after we moved here . . ." I stammered into the phone receiver.

"Yes," a flat voice responded.

"Well, we moved here from a place where libraries don't charge fines."

"Yes," the voice grunted.

Determined, I ignored his lack of enthusiasm. "Well, I checked out too many books, and I didn't mean to, but I kept them too long and when they were overdue I just drove up and dropped them into your night depository and I've never paid and it's been two years and . . ."

I'd completely run out of breath before considering the terrible possibility: Maybe incoming calls are recorded! I should have covered the mouthpiece with a kitchen towel or something! Now they'll probably come and take me away.

I recalled the night (I was in the fifth grade) when I'd tampered with the "Do Not Remove Under Penalty of Law" tags from my mattress. For weeks I'd worried that my mother would find me out.

"You'll have to come in," the library man drawled, as if his mouth were full of pencils and his day filled with people like me.

"Come in?" I yelped, then added, as any thoroughly flustered overdue book offender might, "Oh."

Hanging up, I determined that I'd wait another two, maybe even three years! Maybe we'll be transferred to another part of the country. But when I turned around, my husband stood there holding my coat, mumbling something like, "Come on, I'm taking you in."

"I can't do it," I moaned. "They'll take away my privileges!"

"Take away *what?* You don't have any privileges left! You've been afraid to show your face around there for two years!"

At the desk, not one staff member smiled. I tried to look friendly, but even half a grin seemed beyond me. I turned back toward my tower of strength, but he'd taken off to the place where folks without fines go: card files, microfiche, and the reference desk.

"May I help you?" Both my neck and thoughts snapped back toward the counter.

When I couldn't respond, she repeated herself, but with a softer voice, which startled me even more than her initial tone. She didn't appear soft. I immediately shelved the idea of sharing my long-drawn list of excuses. The truth was, I'd sinned. I told her so. She laughed. My knees ceased shaking, and my queasy stomach rejoiced. I asked her what I had to do to make amends.

"Well, let's just look into the computer and see if you're in there, Miss," she offered.

"Miss," she called me! I felt better immediately. I smiled, patting my salt-and-pepper hair.

"We'll just run it through," she explained, after I'd revealed my complete name and number. "We'll soon know whether we've forgiven you or not."

As I waited, the screen flipped through the names of one card-holder after the other, many of them desperadoes with books out, fines owed.

I gripped the counter and made silent vows: I'll never again check out 12 books when I barely have time for 3, never again mark delinquent notices, "Address Unknown" or "Return to Sender" . . .

"Well, you're in here," the woman chirped.

I didn't want to look, but she was tapping her pencil on the counter. I recalled my second grade teacher, Mrs. Lay. When she'd tapped her pencil, it meant I was on my way to the back of the room, my mouth taped shut while my friends snickered. But I looked. And the librarian smiled.

"There, you're free," she announced.

"Free?"

"Yes." She nodded as she spun the screen toward me. There I saw it: "No books out. No fines owed." Free.

"If it isn't in the computer's memory, it won't be in anyone else's either. We couldn't bring a case against you if we tried." She beamed.

All the way to the card files, I was speechless. Not until I stood in line to check out books did it click: "If it isn't in the computer's memory . . ."

We were nearly home before I spoke.

"All that worry and wrestling for nothing."

"All that worry," my husband said.

"Just like that, forgiven."

"Just like that." He grinned.

"Honey!" I exclaimed. "Do you know what this means? No matter how many times my name comes up on that computer's screen, in its memory there's no history of my past! It's erased! Gone! Non-existent."

As my words touched my inner ear, the tears came. God had gotten through. For years I'd tripped over a part of my past, a memory I had tried to avoid without success. Pastors, friends, and even counselors had repeatedly explained that God both forgave *and* forgot, but I hadn't been able to comprehend it. Tonight, however, I'd actually looked into a memory and seen the proof. And in the seeing, I finally understood: Not only had the library given me full pardon, but my Father had granted me amnesty as well.

Good Morning!
Isn't It a Fabulous Day!

The minute the alarm sounded and the clock radio commenced to sing, my grumbling began. The volume was too high, the bedroom too cold. In that slit where the shades don't quite meet the window's frame, it looked like it was going to be freezing outside as well. And gray.

"Whose big idea was this anyway?" I murmured. "Getting up at six in the morning for a brisk walk?"

"Yours," Scotty said, grinning as he vacated our bed and headed for kerosene heaters and the thermostat in the master bath.

"So, get up," he added, laughing, "and be about your affairs."

Over the hems of blankets and sheets, I could see he was still smiling. About what, may I ask? I silently quizzed, keeping to myself any questions about my mate's mental state. What could be so rib-tickling about abandoning a warm bed and donning mismatched jogging clothes, while sensible couples still snoozed under good down and wool?

"My idea?" I snapped. Actually, he was right. It had been my bright idea to walk daily, shed holiday pounds, tighten up, slim down, feel younger than late-40s again.

At my closet, I yanked exercise clothes from off a hook: faded purple sweats, a black wool Marine Corps shirt, a green turtleneck bought for $1.00 at a secondhand store, and shoes with frayed laces that had to be tied twice if I didn't want to fall on my face. Shoes with scuff marks and, written on their tongues, "The Winner" in royal blue.

"Oh, sure . . . ," I breathed, tugging a rosy red ski hat down over my ears and noting how the popcorn stitch was beginning to deteriorate.

Within minutes we'd closed the back door behind us.

Crossing our lane, I noted every window shade in the neighborhood was drawn.

At the main thoroughfare, no traffic. Who in their right minds would be up and driving in a country described as a "bedroom community," for pity's sake?

At the end of the road, we entered a business park where there are wide streets and a few cars—a spot we'd handpicked for walks, back when summer warmed us and green grass had provided places to stop and sit and rest.

My head down, I watched my feet and, out of the corner of my eye, noted Scotty's steps had more bounce to them than mine.

Rounding a bend for a second go-round, I hunched my shoulders, hoped Scotty noticed I was miserable, stuffed my hands deeper into my pockets, and thought about an ad I'd seen for a health spa where every meal was prepared by chefs. A place where patrons lollygagged, and whirlpools, saunas, and universal gyms did all of the work. I'm sure I could get a manicure. And they'd fix my hair and let me sleep late. But would I ever know such indulgence? Poor me, poor me, poor me.

I formed a pout, glowered at broken glass, and pretended not to hear my spouse, who was asking whether or not I was OK.

"What a lousy day," I grumbled under my breath. I kicked a bottle cap against the curb. "Crummy weather," I broadcast, when, suddenly, we were no longer two but three.

"Good morning!" the third person sang with a wave. "Isn't it a fabulous day!"

"Sure is," my mate returned, nodding his head and allowing an agreeable grin to grow.

A fabulous day? What's so fabulous about . . . ? I tipped my chin up to see who this cheerful voice belonged to and, for the first time, realized a sunrise was beginning to brighten a red barn. Chestnut mares grazed beyond a rail fence. Black and white cows were beginning to wander into a grove of birch. And my tall husband looked very handsome in the early morning, with his blond mustache combed, his blue eyes cheer-filled, and his shoulders wide in his L. L. Bean parka with the hood pitched and folded behind his graying head.

Beyond the woman, I noted other employees exiting a building that houses a company that operates around the clock.

The "Good morning" woman had evidently worked the graveyard shift. In one hand she carried a lunch tote. The other she held above her eyes as she squinted into the morning's radiant birth. "Fabulous! I just love it," she said, planting her feet.

This woman had worked all night. I'd slept in a bed made warm by flannel sheets and a down-filled comforter. This woman was heading for home, perhaps to prepare breakfast for a family who would just be getting out of bed. Scotty had promised me breakfast at the diner, after we'd showered and dressed.

I returned the woman's wave. She drew a deep breath of the morning's fresh air, stepped down off the curb, and entered a packed parking lot.

Beyond us, a sunrise of pinks and oranges and lavender reds filled the horizon.

"Good morning!" I exclaimed as the woman sauntered, smiling, toward an aged car with rust on its fenders and a warped vinyl top.

I squeezed Scotty's hand and squinted into the sun as we dropped down over the shortest slope and headed for the crossroads where we'd return to our lane and home.

"It's an incredibly fabulous day!" I said, looking back over my shoulder at the large-framed woman as she wheeled from the parking lot, a glow on her leathery face and her permed blonde hair catching the sun.

I stared at my seasoned shoes. "Actually, they're not so bad," I said, laughing. "At least they make my feet look small."

I noted the skyline had become flawless in crimson and gold. "Incredible," I said, squeezing my spouse's hand and, with a tug, challenging him to race me home. Grateful to a woman who'd looked beyond herself and caused me to look beyond me.

Just Peanuts

My shopping cart parked midaisle, I blurted, "Only 78 cents?" The newspaper ad I'd read had said something about $1.99, and according to in-store fliers, the peanuts originally sold for $2.99.

I pretended nonchalance, not wanting to draw attention.

"It's the only one marked 78 cents," I mumbled. "Some clerk's goofed."

I fondled a correctly priced jar, deposited it in my basket, then withdrew it reluctantly.

But if I don't take the thing, someone else will, I rationalized. Besides, what's it to a national chain?

I seized the bargain, wrestled, then assured myself it was "an unexpected blessing." Approaching the checkout stations, however, I began to lose ground.

Maybe I *should* return it.

Better yet, my virtuous (devious) self suggested, tell the clerk the real price, and maybe he'll reward you.

Inching forward, I studied the peanuts, squinted toward the checker, and initiated a U-turn. Still, the savings was so appealing. Besides, that pair of nylons I bought here fell apart. They owe me. Smiling, I slipped into line. I was beginning to win.

The salesclerk seemed unusually alert. What if he notices? I shuddered, searching for another line I might slip through more easily.

This is ridiculous, I argued under my breath. *He* doesn't care. *He* still gets his paycheck. My thoughts raced as I crept closer. Besides, if he says anything, I'll play dumb.

One foot nearer to the register, my ears began tingling. I knew they were red. He'll *see* something's up, now. Still, I wormed forward and had nearly touched the target when my husband emerged from Shampoos and grabbed me.

"Hi, Babe." Scotty smiled, slipping his arm around me. "What's up?"

I nearly threw my hands into the air until I realized *he* didn't *know* what was "up." Relaxing, I moved to Plan B.

"Honey, I'm going out front for a rain check. Do these for me?" I nodded toward my cart.

"Yup." Scotty smiled, fetching his wallet. His expression was so innocent, I nearly repented.

"No," I breathed, and spun toward Customer Service, vowing nothing would or could dissuade me.

Meanwhile, my unsuspecting spouse stepped to the counter, paid for my loot, *and* assisted the bagger.

That night my husband slept while I tossed, flopped right, flipped left, opened windows, pulled blankets over my head, monologized, and counted peanuts!

The next day, guests arrived, praised dinner, devoured dessert, but refused the offer of even one nut.

That evening, while clearing dishes, I stared at the four overflowing snack bowls and winced. Overnight, my "treats" had become more than peanuts; they'd become evidence!

The following day, with errands to run, I dismissed "such a small thing." And by the time the sun filtered through the apple trees and into our kitchen, I'd talked myself into believing it was "really no big deal!"

I drove to the post office, skimmed the dime store, gulped lunch, and had raced halfway home when guilt charged me again.

"You haven't done *one* dishonest thing; you've done *two*! Cheated the store *and* made your husband an accomplice."

The rearview mirror revealed that my ears were red again. And, gripping the wheel, I was certain I heard it: one still, small voice.

"With Eve, it was apples."

"No," I argued, "it isn't the same." But, fighting tears, I swerved into the left lane and signaled. I couldn't go home; I had unfinished business.

The girl at the desk was confused. "You're paying $1.21 for peanuts you don't have? You don't have a sales slip and don't want a receipt? You just want to give us $1.21?"

"Yes," I said, nodding vehemently. "The jar was mismarked; they're supposed to be more, I got them for less, and—"

"Well, I'll have to call someone."

"Fine." I pretended to straighten my hair and tried covering my ears.

"Someone" arrived, apparently as dumbfounded as the first girl. I tried to explain: I didn't want *their* peanuts on *my* conscience. They held a miniconference, shrugged several times, and temporarily tuned me out. Eventually, however, they determined where to send me. One girl accompanied me. And I kept thinking, All this over peanuts?

"She wants to give you $1.21," the second girl told a third. I noted puzzled stares, but I didn't say a word. Instead, I fished nervously through my purse and plucked out $1.21 in pennies, nickels, and dimes.

"What am I charging you for?"

Theft, I thought. "Peanuts," I whispered.

"Oh." She paused. "Where are they?"

"Home. I have them at home," I mumbled, backing toward the exit.

"Wait, you'll need a receipt," she yodeled. And then, just about the time I'd made it through the turnstile and into the lobby that would lead to the parking lot, she moaned.

"Oh, no. Rang it up wrong," she said. "Hit $1.22! Not $1.21."

"That's OK!" I exclaimed, snagging another penny from my purse, dashing for the door, feeling free.

That evening, I confessed and endured my husband's laughter. Later, however, as I slipped into bed and leaned toward my spouse, I whispered, "You know, that would make a good story, with a slight twist."

"What?"

"Well, suppose the wife does what I did, her conscience gets to her, and she returns to pay. But, later, she finds the sales slip with *no* 78¢ charge."

"Run that by me again."

"Well, suppose the husband caught it or the clerk or . . ." My pulse accelerated. "Scotty, what *did* you pay for those nuts?"

"Never looked."

"The sales slip?"

"You saved it for some money-back offer. Remember?"

I wouldn't sleep without knowing. At the cupboard, I grabbed the box. The slip was sticking out of one corner. I yanked it and slumped. No 78¢.

Numb, I felt my way back to bed and dropped.

"Know what, Honey?" I croaked. "I paid $1.99 after all."

"No, you didn't," Scotty chuckled. "You paid $3.21 and two nights' sleep." He paused. "You've heard of people getting their 'just desserts'? Well, looks to me like you got your 'just peanuts' too."

Teaching by Example

"I have set you an example that you should do as I have done for you" (John 13:15, NIV).

It was obvious: I needed a computer for my work, *and* my husband was eager to buy just the one for me. However, the "thing" hadn't been unpacked half an hour when I began to cry.

"No way!" I whooped, slamming the owner's manual shut. "It's written in a foreign language! I'm just a housewife! You have a master's degree!" I glowered at the tender grin on my husband's face.

"Babe," Scotty said, "move over so that there's room at that keyboard for a second chair, and let me help." He would, he said, be teaching me something wonderful and new. And he did. He took three days' annual leave with meals in front of the monitor. He walked me through the entire text until I felt ready to write, rewrite, spell-check, and print out.

One month later, a fellow writer called. She bought the same computer. Would I show her how to figure the "thing" out?

At first, I could only laugh. But, because my husband had lovingly served and taught me by example, I also said yes to my friend.

Pride and Plumb Lines

My husband's advice about plumb lines, a level, new razor blades, and cutting a second piece of wallpaper before hanging the first had gone over my head. The plaid did incline slightly, but I was certain I could "fix it."

"Babe," my spouse suggested, poking his head through the door for a third visit, "if you'd just take time to—"

"I know what I'm doing!" I whooped, spinning toward the slimy paper, trying desperately to match it somewhere.

My husband departed, and I was glad. I was beginning to see his point but refused to say so out loud.

With each additional shifty piece, it became more obvious: Things weren't going well.

Over breakfast, Scotty had suggested something about walls not being straight. I'd nodded casually, which meant not agreement but a closed subject.

Now, recalling his earlier warning and noting my room *was* beginning to tilt, I consoled myself. "I'll just hang a few pictures." Chasing several elusive air bubbles, I continued, "Besides, my desk covers half a wall."

I rounded the corner. What had he said about corners? Something about only half-an-inch overlap? I had two inches! "I'll hang a plant," I murmured.

Five hours and four rolls later, the project was finished, and I was ready for "Open House."

Pushing the desk into one defective corner, I hung my plant, grabbed tacks, scrupulously placed my calendar and pictures, shoved the sofa against a wall, strategically positioned my typing table, convinced myself they'd never notice, and called my family.

Our teen slipped through the door as if she were trying her sea legs. "Mom, it's beautiful paper, but . . ." She inspected the wall directly behind me. I'd hoped she wouldn't. "Mom, it's a little crooked, don't you think?"

"No way!" I argued. But as I stepped back and surveyed with an objective, rather than a jaundiced, eye, I knew she was right. Priscillas hadn't covered it. Pictures never would. Figuring I'd hide "a few flaws" somehow, in the corner behind the tall desk, hadn't worked out either. Every attempt I'd made to camouflage had only emphasized imperfections. I'd patched—even employed a blue felt pen where papers refused to meet. But every imperfection I'd tried to mask was highlighted by oddly arranged pictures.

My husband tipped his head to one side and sized up the sloping outer wall. Then he offered a hug.

"I blew it! I really blew it!" I wailed like a lost child in a K-Mart store, pressing my nose against my spouse's chest. "If only I'd listened to you or had let you help when you offered. Now look what I've done. All that money. It's just a waste, *and* I'll be looking at it for years!"

Scotty tipped my chin, leaned his face into mine, and whispered, "Yes, but did you learn anything?"

"Did I *learn* anything?" I mused. "I learned I have too few pictures—and too much pride."

We laughed, but walking from the room, I recalled a proverb, one I kept on my desk in the office in which I'd failed my test: "Hear instruction and be wise, and do not neglect it" (Prov. 8:33, RSV). And I made a vow: The next time I tried taking on a two-man project, I would first line up with that fitting Word. Then I'd be plumb.

The Idol

For years I'd longed for something more elegant than an aging pickup truck. Something for special occasions, dinner, family reunions, church. So when after much planning, praying, and saving, we discovered we were ready to buy a beautiful automobile, I was ecstatic. For days, I dusted, vacuumed, washed, and polished our new possession. I also pleaded with my husband: "Save it for good! Please leave it in the garage until we really need to get it out. The sun and sand might tarnish it. And I love it so much."

"Too much," my entire family chimed.

"If you don't stop worshiping that car, it goes back to the dealer!" my husband said.

"I'm not worshiping any car," I argued. "I just want to keep it looking nice because you've worked so hard and we've saved for so long and—"

"And I want you to take that car out of the garage this morning and drive it to your meeting." My spouse didn't exactly bark an order, but I couldn't deny his words were more mandate than maybe.

I immediately envisioned myself leaving the freeway, bumping along back roads to Donna's, and gathering dust on the shine I'd religiously buffed.

I cringed, considered one last plea, then decided this was one of those occasions when it would be best if I said nothing more at all.

One hour later, I gripped the wheel as if rigor mortis had claimed me. Though my head barely pivoted on my rigid neck, I studied every car ahead to my right and left and in my rearview mirror.

"Keep your distance," I breathed.

Within minutes from our home, I entered the freeway. Morning traffic pressed from all sides. It seemed not one driver was keeping to the posted speed. Even my pulse raced.

"Father," I grumbled, "our car should not be out here. I'm so angry, I have a good notion to head for home. This beautiful thing is just too special for this kind of funny business. Scotty really acted foolishly this time!"

I'd have said more but, suddenly, in the middle of my murmuring, a truck appeared in my mirror, peeled beyond me, and slammed a kernel of rock against my windshield. A cavity about the size of a dime. Perfectly centered, perfectly clear, a defect perfectly level with my eye.

My first reaction was anger. But my surprising second reaction was relief. And, edging off the freeway and into the dirt lane that led to my meeting place, I noted not only an alteration in the windshield but a change in me as well. Tension that had gripped my head and neck no longer tormented me. The fear that had plagued me no longer existed. Scotty hadn't been foolish; the folly had been mine. How ridiculous to have made such an idol of a mere automobile.

"Father, forgive me," I prayed. And, as I did so, I experienced peace. The golden calf would no longer be the object of my affection. God had shattered the graven image, and He'd done so with one small stone.

True Fulfillment

"Remember the words of the Lord Jesus, how he said, It is more blessed to give than to receive" (Acts 20:35, KJV).

Our new house was even smaller than we'd feared. Its one saving grace was the second refrigerator: an enormous side-by-side! I planned to stuff it chock-full after we'd attended a Bible study. We still had no church home. Maybe, tonight, we'd find our niche.

Minutes into the study, we realized this congregation wasn't ours. At its closing, we backed toward the door as the pastor's young wife said, "Could we pray before you go?"

The stove in their rental no longer worked. She cooked on a hot plate for a family of five! She warmed water and bathed her three daughters in a plastic tub. "And," she added, "we need a second picnic cooler." Nothing could be done for their refrigerator.

No! I silently exclaimed. I'm not parting with either of mine!

I traversed the room. My husband held the screen door. We promised we'd pray, but we made it only so far as our car.

"Know what I'm thinking?" I whispered, elbows on the roof, chin in hands.

My husband grinned.

Next morning, the pastor borrowed a truck and claimed his enormous side-by-side. And, watching his three dancing children, I knew: It wasn't simply more blessed to give; it was wonderful fun!

Everywhere I Looked, I Was Afraid

Awakened at 3 A.M. I was immediately alarmed and confused. I groped for my husband, then remembered he was miles away. I was alone.

Questions screamed accusingly: Are the windows closed? Did you lock the doors? Several mornings I'd discovered open windows. More than once I'd forgotten a door.

"How could I be so foolish?" I murmured.

I noted a scraping against the house, outside my study. I'd have cried, but panic paralyzed me.

As I buried my face, a sudden thought commanded, "Get up *now* and read the Word!"

I clutched my pillow. My stomach cramped. Concerned friends had suggested I face my fear. But now?

How can I leave my bed, let alone read? Had anything ever made less sense? Still the nudging persisted, and within seconds I uttered, "What shall I read?"

Instantly the 31st psalm came to mind.

Trembling, I slipped out of bed, and something rustled below the window of the next room, the very room where my Bible waited.

I edged into the black hallway, where fear of the dark met me. "Lord, how can I turn on lights, sit, and read if someone *is* out there?"

Flipping the light switch, I fled to the sewing machine for scissors. Terror gripped me as I seized the shears. I dropped to the couch, my weapon in one hand, my Bible in the other.

As my pulse raged, my neck tightened, and my jaws locked, I considered the cliché "scared to death." I determined I wouldn't take my eyes off the psalm. Sensing I was to read the words *aloud,* I also vowed, with some trepidation, to follow "directions" no matter what.

Again, bushes whispered.

I wondered if I should call the police. I'd phoned them so *often.* Each time, they'd responded with kindness. But I just wouldn't chance embarrassment again.

Recalling that "faith cometh by hearing, and hearing by the word of God" (Rom. 10:17, KJV), I read—aloud.

"Lord, I trust in you alone. Don't let my enemies defeat me," the Psalmist began (31:1, all TLB). "Be for me a great Rock of safety from my foes" (v. 2). My heart rate moved into high gear as, behind the shade and within my imagination, a lurking figure took shape.

Again, fear nearly overwhelmed me. Is there *actually* a human outside? A month earlier we *had* discovered footprints. On another occasion a man, or perhaps a teen, *had* been spotted near our cars. But the police had checked all the way to the woods and found no one. Days later, our daughter told us she thought a boy had been playing a joke on her. I imagined otherwise.

Now I wondered, Has he come through a window? Is he at the other end of the house? Behind me? In the hall?

Disabled by fright, I couldn't even turn my own head! I'm trapped in a room with no phone and no second exit!

"Yes, you are my Rock and my fortress; honor your name by leading me out of this peril," the Psalmist wrote (v. 3).

"What peril?" I nearly screamed. My fingers wrapped around the scissors.

"Pull me from the trap my enemies have set for me. For you alone are strong enough. Into your hand I commit my spirit" (vv. 4-5). My ears remained "on alert," but my body relaxed somewhat as I considered God's strength *and* refused to imagine footsteps or a bumping against the window wall.

"You have rescued me, O God who keeps his promises" (v. 5).

Yes, I thought, recalling other crises, other saves.

I continued reading until my voice miscarried over the words "For you have listened to my troubles and have seen the crisis in my soul" (v. 7).

"Where?" I breathed.

"In my soul," the Psalmist had written.

For several seconds I read nothing, whispered nothing as I tried to comprehend the Psalmist's words and their application to my present situation.

Could it be, I wondered, that the Lord assigned this reading not because a threat lurks under my window but because a crisis threatens within my soul? Admittedly, I'd walked, talked, and considered fear even as I'd prepared for bed. Had my words and thoughts taken root in my spirit?

"Lord," I whispered, "is that the *real* crisis?"

His answer came from His Word hidden within. "For as he thinketh in his heart, so is he" (Prov. 23:7, KJV).

My ears continued detecting odd noises I might have identified as footsteps except for the fact that my staying in the Word had begun to renew my mind, my trust, and my courage.

"Everywhere I looked I was afraid" (v. 13), an apt description of my first thoughts and actions. "But I was trusting you, O Lord" (v. 14).

I recalled that raccoons and possums had been sighted prowling around our neighborhood, and I relaxed a bit more. I asked God to forgive me for my slow progress, though I believed He understood. That my getting out of bed and into His Word had been the way to victory.

"What time I am afraid, I will trust in thee" (56:3, KJV).

I drew a deep breath and started over, determined I'd read until I was set completely free. I believed undivided trust would come as I read.

I read, "You alone are my God; my times are in your hands" (vv. 14-15).

After several readings, my eyes fixed on "times." I glanced at the clock; I'd read for more than an hour! Daylight sifted through priscillas. The only sound was the owl's good-night.

I wriggled my toes into the soft, green carpet. I smiled and it felt good.

"For you have stored up great blessings for those who trust and reverence you," I read (v. 19).

I've already experienced several of those blessings, I thought with a laugh, noting that my shoulders had relaxed, tension had released its grip on my neck, and fear had withdrawn.

Delivered at last from the tormentors, I suppressed a yawn and skimmed to the end of the psalm.

"So cheer up! Take courage if you are depending on the Lord" (v. 24).

Yes, it takes courage to be a woman so often alone, I agreed. But I'll never look for it in a pair of long-handled scissors again.

I tapped the cushion beside me. The shears weren't there. I searched behind pillows, under my robe's hem, and between couch cushions. Finally, my fingers touched the metal of my truant shield, and I laughed.

"Some protection," I said.

Several weeks later, my faith was tested again. My husband was away; so was our daughter. Around midnight, thunder and lightning rocked our entire township. Trees fell. Roof shingles lifted. Houses were struck. Every outlet in our house popped and sizzled and snapped!

Storms had always terrified me. However, that night I sipped tea, listened to music, and read. Occasionally, I did detect creaks and groans inside the house, but I simply considered my Father's Word and boldly exclaimed, "I am not afraid!"

Divine Vision

"And the Lord said, I have surely seen the affliction of my people which are in Egypt, and have heard their cry by reason of their task-masters; for I know their sorrows" (Exod. 3:7, KJV).

We longed for familiar surroundings, friendships, family, roots. My husband had been promised a promotion to the very spot where we'd met and married. Where he'd grown up. Where much of his family still lived. A land of milk, and honey too. Now they'd promoted someone else. We wouldn't be going home after all.

It seemed more than we could handle. Why had the Lord led us to words promising He'd given us the city? Told us to go home to our friends and tell them what wonderful things He'd done for us? Why had one door after another opened, only to have this final one slam shut?

Once, we'd believed we preferred not to return to a ranching community without exquisite dining, professional sports, and novelties too numerous to count. But the Lord himself seemed to have changed our minds and fired us with this one desire.

It didn't make sense, we repeatedly cried out, until the day we acknowledged God hadn't said "when" or "how." We hadn't been misled by His Spirit nor by His Word. He had given us a vision for home.

Today we still believe we will see ourselves delivered. It's simply a matter of waiting on and trusting Him.

There's a Promise in the Mountains

Often I had affectionately suggested that my husband's disposition resembled a St. Bernard's. So when he began to change radically, to become irritable and agitated over matters I viewed as trivial, I was confused.

I really couldn't blame him for being somewhat anxious. Transferred from the Northwest to New Mexico, we worried about our midschooler's adjustment. There also were financial demands: braces for Lisa's teeth, a home more costly than expected, and the need for a second car. Still, I wondered if his mood had resulted from something I'd said.

By week's end, we were sharing little or nothing with one another. Rather than snap, bark, or accuse, each stayed out of the other's way. For us, this strain was foreign. We'd never gone to bed angry, seldom allowed discord to fester.

On Sunday, I sat in church thinking, What a farce. Seated here smiling, praising, and praying. If they only knew.

I longed to go home where I might wail before the Lord; but just as I toyed with the thought of bolting, I glanced across the sanctuary and out at the towering hills.

"There's a promise in the mountains," the Lord seemed to say.

What could that mean? I wondered. Did it suggest that in all difficult situations there's distant good? I couldn't see any good coming from too many bills and too little cash. What was so good about a car needing new tires about the time we'd worked out a three-year payment plan to deal with dental bills?

Offering baskets interrupted my musing, and I murmured, "I'd like to be on the receiving end of that collection. Just once."

Again, the "still, small voice" whispered, "There's a promise in the mountains." But I ignored the prompt. My overtaxed spirit had given up.

By the end of the service, I was down. My husband hadn't softened, hadn't taken my hand when I'd touched his sleeve, hadn't smiled.

After church we drove in silence. But for aging-car splutters, you could have heard a butterfly's wings. Not until we inched into our driveway did my spouse speak.

"Do you have to correct papers?" he asked, his voice husky.

"Well, I should . . . but I'm flexible," I said. I'd taken work as a substitute teacher. I worried about falling behind. But the look on my husband's face kept me from saying so.

"How about I pack lunch while you change? Then we'll hike into the mountains," he said.

Bells didn't ring, but my spirit nearly sang as the mountain thoughts once again nudged.

Revived, I raced to my closet, dressed in minutes, and returned to the kitchen where I found my husband—silent, again.

Deflated, I pressed against my car door and rode to the head of the trail, where my husband began hiking without one word.

For three miles we said nothing, then Scotty suddenly sat down and said flatly, "Let's eat."

Cramped and confused, I knelt on the grass and touched my husband's hand. "Honey, what is it?" I asked. "Can't I help?"

That's when I saw his tears.

"I didn't want to upset you, but the Lord's been dealing with me," he said. His shoulders slumped. I expected the worst.

"And?"

"We're to double our giving."

Truth is, I nearly flipped! "Did He tell you *how?*" I blurted.

"No," Scotty said.

"What'll we do?" I groaned.

"Double our giving." My husband's words were direct and punctuated by the first hug I'd received in days.

After sketchy conversation, we hiked. I saw relief in my husband's stride, but by the time we'd reached the summit, I was angry. Scotty needed suits for work; Lisa wanted clothes for school; I hadn't had a new dress in several years; I couldn't remember our last dinner out.

That evening my husband was once again himself, but I was overwhelmed, and I retreated to my knees.

"How?" I wept.

"By an act of your will," the Lord impressed.

"When?"

"Now."

"Why?"

"Because I want to bless you."

I had nothing more to say. It was now between my spouse and the Lord.

The following week we doubled our giving; and I can't tell you how, but within weeks there were dresses, dinners out, work clothes for my husband, *and* even skating for Lisa.

No, Scotty didn't get a raise. But, somehow, after bills, there was money for us and a lesson for me: In all of life's mountains there are promises. I may not always understand, but if I'll do it God's way, those promises will surely come to pass.

That nothing more to see it was just to see... and the others.

Then finally, when we looked and found our place and I sat low... into the cushions there were the seats with our worn out...
I'm comforted, and was staring and I too...

Well - my father got a car that morning there are all those who remember and a lesson he taught about the... meant... they do remember too, the driver to whom... to S.M.W. for that time it was perhaps a young woman remembering.

PART 2

FOR MOTHERS

"He settles the barren woman in her home as a happy mother of children. Praise the Lord."

Ps. 113:9, NIV

Person-to-Person, Calling God

"Mom! Everything's a mess!" It was my youngest, living away from home for the first time and frustrated because one college roommate or another was "fussy" about one thing or another.

"I'm trying, Mom. I really am. But some of the girls just aren't used to sharing space, and they sleep late and they never pick up after themselves and I go to put on my favorite sweater and someone has it and it's already left the house. *You've* got to pray!"

"Honey, I am praying," I consoled. "But you can pray, too, you know, and talk things out with your friends. Or have you thought of that?"

"Yes, Mom. I've tried talking and I have prayed. But it's not the same. I need *you* to pray for me."

So, long distance and collect, I prayed. This pleased Lisa (and the telephone company), but it disturbed me.

"Mom! You've got to pray right away!" It was my son, also miles away and long distance. He'd graduate soon. It was time to make a job decision. He needed wisdom.

"Well, Rob, you know I'm praying, but God wants to guide *you.*"

"I know, Mom, but . . ."

And so it went. They called and I prayed. I also stewed. Yes, I was thrilled that my children understood God answered prayer, understood we could take any kind of problem to Him. However, one day I realized why I felt perplexed: My children didn't yet understand *their* prayers (minus their mother's amen) carried weight.

"God isn't more stirred by my petitions than by yours," I later explained to Lisa.

"But, Mom, Rob says you have a 'hot line to heaven'!"

"Wait one minute," I said. "God hears every believer's prayer."

Some sort of hot line? Where in the world did they get such notions? And how could I convince them to make their requests known to God, not to their mother?

On the other hand, I had read, "Where two or three are gathered in my name, there I am in the midst of them" (Matt. 18:20, RSV). Maybe my children just didn't feel they had two or three to gather together at their end of the line.

One afternoon, when the house was quiet and I needed a time-out, I picked up my Bible and read, "Train up a child in the way he should go, and when he is old he will not depart from it" (Prov. 22:6, RSV).

Could it be, though they were about to embark on paths of their own, I was still in the business of training up my children? I pictured my son, two heads taller than I. And my daughter, nearly old enough to become a bride. But did I expect too much from my fledglings? Was I trying to push them into flight and private prayer prematurely?

Again I searched the Scriptures and discovered a passage that began to assure me.

Just before Peter's denial, Jesus was trying not only to comfort His disciples but also to explain, "If you had known me, you would have known my Father also." But Philip piped up with, "Lord, show us the Father, and we shall be satisfied" (John 14:7, 8, RSV).

And what was Jesus' response? He patiently pointed out how long they'd known Him. There's no indication He became exasperated with them, even though these men had walked, talked, dined, and lodged with Him.

As I reread the passage, I began to consider my recent protests. If Jesus understood that His disciples were still growing, couldn't I be satisfied with my children's progress? Weren't their requests sufficient evidence God was working in them?

Several nights later, Lisa called again. This time it was not only roommate dilemmas but also the flu.

"You've got to pray for me, Mom! I don't have time for this stress *or* this bug! I have work and classes and things!"

I was tempted to ask about the "things," but I prayed instead. And, later, I confided in a friend.

"I want my children to discover they can pray anytime and anywhere without their mother!"

"I know that," Donna said, "and I feel the same about my offspring. But don't be so impatient. They've seen God answer their mother's prayers, so, of course, they call their mother. But you just wait. It won't be long before they'll figure out God's in the business of answering their private petitions as well."

Not two weeks later, Donna's prophecy came to pass.

First, I heard from Rob. He'd met several Christians, had done some sharing, and prayed. And, sensing God's leading, he'd taken a job.

I was both delighted *and* relieved. But I hadn't heard from Lisa in days. Odd, I thought. So I called her.

"Honey, I've been a little worried. Is everything all right?"

"Well, it is *now*," she said, breathing a weighty, audible sigh.

"Now? What do you mean, *'now'*?" I knew my voice had shifted to its highest pitch, but I didn't care. My daughter's "now" seemed to say my child had *needed* me, and all my motherly instincts began to spring forth.

"Well, it was nothing . . . I guess."

"You *guess*? Lisa?" My pulse accelerated while my daughter prolonged the suspense, disclosing one fragment of her "nothing" at a time.

"Well, see, all of us in the room are getting along fine now, but I've been having some other kinds of trouble, Mom." Again she sighed, the drama of the moment apparently more to her liking than to mine.

"And?" I struggled for composure but heard my voice crack.

"It's homesickness again, and I've been thinking about changing schools, and this man followed me home from work one night, and I have this chest cold, and the dentist says I may need a root canal—"

My gasp, followed by raspy short breaths, terminated Lisa's narrative midspeech.

"Mom? What's wrong?"

"What's wrong?" Again my voice sang out across the wires like the cries of a cat with his tail in the door. "What do you mean, 'What's wrong?' Why didn't you call? I could have prayed!"

She denied it later, but I heard what I heard: My daughter laughed.

"Mom," she said, like a mother soothing a child, "I nearly did call 'collect.' But then I got to thinking about what you said in your last letter about my needing to talk with God personally. Remember? So . . ." She sighed with a hint of contentment, sounding a bit more like a woman than a child. "I called Him 'person-to-Person' instead."

Greener Pastures

My husband was out of town for several days. My husband is more often out of town than in. It's his work. He can't help it. That's just the way it is. But I was feeling sorry for myself.

Then there were the lonesome feelings for the kids. Because of my husband's work, the two of us had been relocated to the East Coast. Three thousand miles from home, three children, and one new son-in-law.

And there was the matter of friends I'd left behind in New Mexico, Montana, and Washington State. Though I'd met women in our new location, it hadn't been easy because of my work. You can't attend luncheons, learn counted cross-stitch, run and play with a host of folks, and still write full-time. Writing must be done in solitary. Loneliness is often a side effect.

This particular morning, I felt I'd had more than my share of seclusion. Still, I had deadlines to meet. I didn't feel free to call someone, make plans, and gallivant. Besides, I was pleased to have been given an assignment. On the other hand, after two hours of murmuring, it seemed to me I was abused and that every other woman I knew had life better than I. Those were my feelings *before* the phone rang.

It was Mabel. "I don't know what I'm going to do." She sighed.

"What's the problem?" I asked.

"George. Just retired, you know. I don't know what I'm going to do with him! He's at my heels *all day long!* Wants to know what he should do with himself. Wants to know if I have anything for him to do for me. Wants to know if it's time to eat. Will I go look at garden seeds? I think I'll scream!"

Mabel, too, is a writer. She, too, is pedaling as fast as she can, hoping to make a deadline, and also hoping to complete a book while there's still interest at the publisher's end and "energy enough to persevere."

We talked. I told her, yes, I would pray both for her *and* for her husband. "He needs time to figure out how to change speeds," I suggested. Then I realized I'd never been in Mabel's shoes and refrained from saying anything more.

Mabel closed the conversation, saying she *did* understand her husband's needs, but it was "just so frustrating some days."

Replacing the receiver, I thought, Maybe my situation could be worse. Still, what I wouldn't give to have my spouse around a bit more . . .

My monologue was interrupted by another call. This time it was Betty.

"Nanc', I need prayer!" Her request was more of a shriek. It surprised me. Betty is soft-spoken and calm. But this morning she sounded like a 747 revving up!

"What's the matter?" I asked.

"Kids! Everywhere! I have Bible study. I don't want to miss out again, but I can't go unprepared. And I finally have an assignment. That sailing piece. You know, the one I thought I'd never sell? Well, the editor wants it. Now! But the kids, every one of them, decided this was the week to come see us. Brought their kids *and* a dog. They're sleeping all over the house . . . late. I'm fixing three breakfasts. The baby cried all night. Help!"

We talked. We prayed. And as my friend completed her sharing, I realized I wouldn't exactly want to take her place. Still, as I hung up the receiver, I thought, On the other hand, Betty doesn't know what it's like not to have . . .

Again the phone sounded. It was amazing to me. In our home, where the phone maybe rings once a day, to have a third call before nine o'clock!

It was Donna. I was glad. Donna always understood. The other two hadn't let me get a word in, except to pray for *their* needs. But Donna would listen while I told her how down I felt and how much I missed my kids. At least, that's what I thought until she explained the reason for her call.

"Would you believe I have a luncheon to set up by noon? I have to stay until the fellowship hall's clean. Then, this evening, I'm serving the missionary supper. Yesterday there was a going-away lunch for a neighbor and a makeup class at the club. And tomorrow, Frank wants me to prepare the guest room for three boys passing through from Guam. I have really had it!"

I heard what my friend was saying, heard her distress, and knew she needed to talk and pray. But I also heard God's "still, small voice." So, while my friend chattered, I listened to the Lord.

My situation, absence of husband and children and old friends, was not my wilderness experience as I'd frequently remarked. I was exactly where I needed to be for what I needed to do. Yes, there were days when I missed my husband, but the Lord had said, "For your Maker is your husband—the Lord Almighty is his name" (Isa. 54:5, NIV). Some days I longed to be surrounded by children, but the Lord had said, "Train a child in the way he should go . . ." (Prov. 22:6, NIV). Mine had gone, but they'd come to know Him. And friends? Well, true, I missed the ones I'd left behind, and from time to time I longed to dawdle over lunch or spend hours with flocks of familiar folks. But as I concluded my conversation and put away the phone, the Lord nudged once more with a promise from His Word.

"A man of many companions may come to ruin, but there is a friend who sticks closer than a brother" (Prov. 18:24, NIV).

As I entered my office, a poster gift from a friend caught my eye. Four cows grazed, each in separate but identical pastures, joined at the center of the page. Barbed wire fenced each grazing area. Ample grass surrounded each cow. But cow No. 1 ate in pasture No. 2, her neck stretched through wire, her tongue straining for every last blade. Cow No. 2 dined in pasture No. 3. Cow No. 3 had poked her head so far into pasture No. 4 she was nearly on hoof tips. And, of course, cow No. 4 had obviously decided cow No. 1's pasture was the best she'd ever seen!

Yes, the picture is humorous. But it also reminds me that Mabel and Betty and Donna taught me something I needed to know: Their pastures are no greener than mine.

The Impression Maker

I'd sensed God's nudging and acknowledged days did go better when I began them with prayer and devotions; but today, I rationalized, is different. This morning I have other plans.

My son, Robert, had arrived for his first visit since our move to the Northeast, where I'd learned to drive a tractor. And, childish or not, I planned to show off. Prayer would have to wait.

I recalled Robert's excitement when we'd taken the training wheels off his bike, and he'd flown down the hill with his best friend, Ray. True, they'd been preschoolers, whereas I was now over 40. However, I mused, even at my age I have a right to be proud of such an accomplishment.

I'd anticipated and planned since daybreak. After breakfast, I'd saunter to the garage, slip into the tractor seat, flip the ignition, and amaze him. However, as I scraped dishes and pictured how impressed my son would be when he realized I was capable of more than cookie baking, tole painting, and piano duets (while he tackled the most difficult parts), Robert stepped into the kitchen, hugged me, and announced he was taking his sister shopping.

Oh, no, I thought. Just when I'm all set? My husband had tuned the engine, checked the steering, and filled the tank and tires.

Well, I reasoned, the kids are getting an early start, and I'm running late. They'll still catch me as I just happen to be mowing. Secretly I prayed, *"Please* let them come back in time."

The morning air was perfect. The sun was slowly burning the dew from the lawn. By the time the grass dried, I was certain Robert would tire of Lisa's shopping.

I donned my red-and-yellow fishing hat, my husband's Marine Corps shirt, Robert's ragged hand-me-down denims, and Lisa's sneakers (donated to my wardrobe because they were no longer in).

Peering into the hall mirror, I smiled: "Perfect. Exactly the impression I'm after."

Two hours into the mowing, my children hadn't returned. "Surely Robert's given up by now," I muttered. "Lisa can be a pill when she's shopping."

I rounded the far end of our property. I surveyed the road beyond our neighbor's stone barn. I saw no one.

"Lord," I pleaded aloud, as I chugged up the steep slope toward our front porch, "I'll be done soon, and Rob won't have seen me drive this tractor!"

"Wouldn't you rather have him come home and catch you reading your Bible?"

Instantly my mouth parched as I considered the possibility that that sudden idea had not been my own. Determined, however, I dismissed the nagging question, leaned forward, and urged the reluctant vehicle up our hill. Then it happened.

Groaning and sliding on slimy grass, the tractor began backing downhill sideways! Pictures flashed through my mind of the day this same machine had turned over on my husband, and he'd miraculously escaped. The memory panicked me. I shifted into the *wrong* gear. The motor responded. The tractor lurched!

I gripped the wheel, my hat slipped down over one ear, I tried to save my glasses, one leg kicked air involuntarily as I struggled to maintain my balance, and then I slammed into the post that supports our outdoor lamp!

As I struck it, the post moaned toward the driveway on the downhill side. I immediately threw my right foot into action. That is, I tried.

"The brake!" I bawled. "Where's the brake?" One squint and my question was answered: It was hooked around the lamp's column and, as a result, I couldn't press my foot on the brake *or* the clutch!

The motor expelled both smoke streams and howls. Metal against metal resembled fingernails on chalkboard. But the sound wasn't quite enough to disguise the one from the driveway.

Fumbling for the ignition switch and twisting the key to "off," I knew even before turning my head: The blast came from our Datsun's horn. The laughter was my son's. As I'd prayerfully requested, he had come home.

Leaning against the car, Robert howled until tears ran down his face while my daughter, embarrassed for me, explained, "Even though she sometimes does things like that, she really is all there." However, for nearly one week, every time my son looked at me, he cupped his hand over his mouth, pinched, and grinned.

Meanwhile, as soon as I'd pulled the machine off the post (which required assistance) and shoved the lamp to a nearly upright position, I stumbled to the shower on wobbly legs, tugged on fresh clothing, and occupied myself at last with devotions, my Bible, and prayer. And though I was later than usual, I had the distinct impression God hadn't missed even a minute. He'd been right on time.

A Message for Kathy

There was no doubt about it. That feeling in the pit of my stomach was fear.

This just isn't like me, I thought, as I pushed open the glass door of the cafeteria where the dinner meeting was to be held.

Earlier in the day I'd spoken to another women's group and had enjoyed it so much I'd practically flown the 50 miles back to Albuquerque. The earlier reception had been warm and responsive, the atmosphere friendly and loving. I'd felt relaxed and in tune with the audience from the very beginning.

But now my apprehension mounted as the hostess for the evening spotted me, introduced herself with a firm, businesslike handshake, then quickly propelled me through the cafeteria food line, explaining she didn't want to "hold up the evening's schedule."

Seated at the head table, old insecurities taunted as the hostess, her back to me, carried on a discussion with a fellow officer. I felt isolated and rejected.

While I mentally reviewed my note cards, I glanced around the room at the audience of professional women who were showing obvious signs of restlessness and fatigue after having spent a full day at work. I saw little indication that my message would be well received by even one woman in that room.

The subject was child abuse and God's power to heal the most painful memories. I wanted to affirm that even an unwanted child could become whole in Christ and move on to a renewed, restored, joy-filled life.

While cutting my roast beef, I sent up an urgent prayer. "Lord, did I jump into this one on my own? Have I accepted an invitation *You* did not approve? Please, Lord, help!"

I pushed cold peas and carrots from one side of the plate to the other. I didn't hear one word from the Lord.

The evening wore on. A rendition by a local opera singer and a lengthy craft demonstration did little to rouse the women from their lethargy.

I was becoming desperate. "Lord, please get me out of here," I pleaded, "or give me a new message. The women are tired. The temperature outside is still 95 degrees, and they're obviously in no mood to listen to sobering reflections."

Again I heard only the Lord's silence, and I mentally bolted for the door—just as the hostess introduced the main speaker: me.

I had no choice but to plunge into the speech I'd prepared.

It didn't take long before I knew, however, that I'd guessed correctly: The women were bored. Several yawned and shifted in their chairs; others stared at the clock. But within minutes, I discovered I didn't really care whether they were listening or not. I knew, without knowing the reason why, my subject had been selected by the Lord; and, in obedience, I was going to share every word of it before I stepped down from that stage.

Undergirded now, I began to speak boldly. I also began to sense the Holy Spirit's participation as I rushed to say it all within my allotted time.

I stressed that no matter what physical or emotional hurts we may have suffered at the hands of family, Scripture tells us, "When my father and my mother forsake me, then the Lord will take me up" (Ps. 27:10, KJV).

I reminded the audience that God had planned my birth and that He'd planned theirs as well.

"All of us were 'wanted' children. None of us were 'disappointments' to Him when we came into this world.

"I am His beloved." I rejoiced and reminded them they were beloved, too, though I doubted anyone heard as they wrapped coats around their shoulders, clamored for purses, and folded programs with a flare.

Then, just as I'd begun to relax and moved to pray, the hostess flipped a note in front of my face.

"Time's up!"

My mouth dropped open, the hostess stepped to the microphone, and the meeting was closed.

But for stubborn pride, I would have cried. Instead, I returned to my table and prepared for a quick exit, while angrily complaining to God, "Why did You lay such a message on my heart?"

I scooped up my belongings and felt a timid tap on my arm.

As I turned, I saw the glowing, tear-streaked face of a young girl. What was a new teen doing at a businesswomen's gathering?

Half smiling and half crying, she introduced herself as Kathy. She told me she had been abused. She'd finally run away from home, but because a Christian teacher cared, she'd been placed with the teacher's family and introduced to the Lord.

Her eyes were shining. "They told me, in my new family, that God really loves me," she said. And He'd confirmed it tonight.

I was speechless.

To the side stood Kathy's foster mother, a gentle Christian woman who'd felt led to bring her new daughter to the meeting, even though it wasn't generally done.

She wrapped a protective arm around Kathy as she told me how close she'd come to leaving her at home that evening.

We hugged and laughed and shared. I told them how I'd tried to convince the Lord to give me a different message. Our rejoicing turned to awe. It seemed God had planned the entire evening just for a child.

Smiling at Kathy, I could see a healing had begun.

"Thank you for not changing your message," Kathy's new mother called back over her shoulder, as they moved across the room.

"Thank You, Lord," I prayed, "for not permitting me to do so. And thank You, too, for showing me: You are the Worker of wonders, even through a reluctant voice."

My Serve

One Sunday, during my morning devotions, I read, "Your attitude must be like my own, for I, the Messiah, did not come to be served, but to serve" (Matt. 20:28, TLB). Instantly I jotted in my prayer journal, "I see God's desire to make His children leaders, but first, each of us needs a servant's attitude." Then, ignited with the desire to become a leader, I added, "Lord, make *me* a servant."

By Monday, however, my enthusiasm waned as I faced laundry, grocery shopping, my daughter's dental appointment, a newly planted lawn that had to be kept wet, typing for our women's group, ironing, and three full baskets of folding.

By late afternoon, I'd barely finished my chores and errands and had just begun to roll out a crust for cheese pie when my spouse walked into my kitchen one hour early *and* hungry.

I tried to hide my frustration and hoped not to appear totally frazzled, but silently I screeched!

Meanwhile, my agitated teen dashed through the kitchen yelling, "Where's my work uniform? Didn't you iron it yet?"

Seconds later, my spouse squeezed in, "What's for dinner?" The dog whined and wiggled at the back door. I tripped over the scatter rug, pushed the whiner out, slammed the screen, pretended my family was momentarily nonexistent, and pivoted toward a finger-printed window pane.

Glowering at the grackles devouring grass seed I'd toiled over for hours, I furiously whipped eggs and shrieked, "I feel just like a servant!"

As my words pealed, I dropped the wire whip. "I don't believe what I just said!" I exclaimed. Reluctantly smiling, I shook my head and aloud, mused, "Well, Father, it seems when I take *You* at *Your* word, You take *me* at *mine*."

Turning toward my husband to offer and to receive a hug, I requested forgiveness for my nasty-nag attitude. I calmly explained where my daughter's uniform waited—where *she'd* left it. I thanked God for immediate answers to earnest prayer, and I added, "Father, forgive me when I grumble like an unbelieving drudge. Teach me, instead, to celebrate my serve. Amen."

One Family's Meeting

When a single parent remarries, he or she has (I would hope) taken time to make this decision. Such a parent is undoubtedly filled with enthusiasm and expectation and is looking forward to a second chance.

It's not necessarily so, however, for the children.

Twelve years ago, I brought to my second marriage a preteen who adored the man I dated while we dated. She even seemed thrilled about our decision to marry, telling her teachers, "Mom and I are marrying Scotty."

But when we actually came together as a family, it didn't take long to conclude that my daughter had some misgivings about the new arrangement. That Lisa was unhappy wasn't always obvious; that she meant to do some testing was immediately clear.

Before long, Lisa was frequently announcing, "You're not my *real* dad!" Or she'd declare, "I never asked for this wedding!" Then she'd confide in me about "him" or run to "him" about me. And it became obvious to both my husband and me that if our union was going to be all that we hoped, we would have to see to our family, first. But how?

My husband suggested a "family meeting."

I admit I thought (though I never said so out loud) the idea was a little corny. Raised on a cattle ranch, Scotty had been a boy, a man, and a wrangler of dudes. He'd never been a little girl, had never been a dad. What could he know? But we initiated the meeting anyway and immediately began sharing, groping, and growing.

Occasionally, Lisa protested. "Yuck! Not another dumb meeting!" But we held our ground, believing a casual attitude would convey casual concern. Believing, also, if we focused on her concerns, Lisa would know we cared, even when we pulled it off clumsily.

Meetings were called when they were needed, as situations arose that were best handled as a family. They were roundtable discussions, not battleground encounters. We (the "we" included Lisa) were completely free to speak. We also pledged to listen. Listening, however, carried with it certain risks. On occasion, we learned some things about ourselves—things we hadn't exactly wanted to know.

In addition to openness, we were committed to rules.

Rule one: We wouldn't berate or attack; we each had a right to own our own feelings. We began with *"I believe"* or *"I feel."* Not *"You did"* or *"You are."* There was no name-calling: "Fuddy-duddy" wasn't allowed; neither was "Kids today!" Covert manipulation was outlawed, overt dictation banned.

Rule two: We wouldn't interrupt to defend ourselves *or* to referee. There were moments when I was tempted because my family had tried to set me up as the middleman. But we all three agreed early on that I would not be pressed into service. If we hadn't made that decision, our new family arrangement might have become a no-win affair.

We encouraged Lisa to tell how and what she felt. We believed we were to hear what our daughter valued even if those values differed from our own. We included her in our decision making. We let her know our feelings and why we'd ruled as we had. We apprised her of our finances. If we had to say no because of a lack of money, Lisa was encouraged to understand. She didn't always fathom what we were talking about. But then, that's what the meetings were all about: learning to comprehend.

In the beginning, Lisa expressed confusion, resentment, dismay, and even anger. That she loved us both she continually expressed; but she also had other memories, other ties, and hurts that would require time. She showed us we needed to give her that time. She also taught us how to develop her trust: by allowing her to express openly without fear of reprisal. Scotty and I saw ourselves as Lisa's support system; we couldn't think for her, but we could help her sort her thoughts.

In addition, my husband and I didn't cover up the occasional conflicts between us, conflicts that arose because we were in our mid-30s and very much set in our ways. We simply explained to Lisa, "We're having a difference of opinions." We discovered the explanation was absolutely necessary because, in the back of Lisa's mind, there was a fear that *division* spelled *divorce.* She needed to learn that two people who love one another can discuss differences and build a strong marriage based on care-filled confrontation.

Rule three: If any of us saw, during the course of the meeting, that we had erred, we admitted it. That rule proved most trying for the adults in the house. I recollect some throat clearing, wrestling, and silence. But eventually we got that rule together too. And when we did, Lisa did likewise.

It took time, but we became a family. My spouse assumed his rightful position as head of the home. I relaxed, knowing my husband

58

and child loved one another. Mutual respect developed, and the three of us did some growing up. One day we began to notice that our daughter, without stress or confusion, had learned to confront others as well.

In sixth grade, Lisa met her atheistic science teacher head-on. She stayed after school, stated her beliefs, accepted his challenge to do her own research, and received an A+ for the course—even after producing a biblically based, faith-filled paper. In high school, when girlfriends disagreed, Lisa proposed, "Let's talk about it." And several years later, when a boy needed to be told there could never be a lifetime tie, our daughter was able to say what had to be said. Today, Lisa's a college senior—one with a mind of her own and willingness to express it.

I'm not saying we've been able to avoid bitter days or bedlam altogether. We've had some rocky crossings, days when we all three wondered if our family would pass the test and fly.

One day (early on in our relationship), I even left home. I'd refused to referee. Doubting I'd ever understand either member of the feud, I gave up and was gone for more than an hour. But, by the time I returned, Scotty had donned coveralls and was building a playhouse for "his girl." And the child I'd labeled a tyrant was fixing dinner and bragging to a friend that her dad was "the best!"

The Word says, "Train a child in the way he should go, and when he is old he will not turn from it" (Prov. 22:6, NIV). Now I confess I've sometimes had my doubts. But today, my husband and I see our Lisa confronting without fear and making positive decisions, choices that seem to be leading to a marriage where daily a family will be meeting.

When Words Cannot Express

It was nearly midnight, but I couldn't sleep. I longed to talk with the Lord, but I had nothing to say. I felt grief-stricken but couldn't pinpoint the source of my pain.

I drank warm milk, wandered through the silent house, considered the Scriptures, but realized I was too distracted to read.

Finally, unable to understand my feelings and uncertain how to express myself to the Lord, I simply entered my office and knelt in the dark, where, just as soon as my knees touched the floor, I began to weep.

Within seconds, my near-silent cry became a sob interspersed with great gulps for air. As I wept, I felt He was not only listening but wholly understanding the heart of me. I felt, too, that as He listened, I was pouring out longings, sharing an old hurt that hadn't fully healed, expressing my longings for my children (who live nearly 3,000 miles away).

I thought, as I cried, how much I missed my oldest daughter. Recently married and away from her phone so much of the time, I hadn't spoken to her in more than two months.

The tears spilled for 5 or 10 minutes. When they subsided, I still had not spoken a word. I hadn't "heard" the Lord. But I had experienced nearness, and I had received peace.

The following morning, we'd barely finished breakfast when the phone rang. It was my daughter, my eldest.

"Mom!" she exclaimed. "I'm so glad I finally got you. I've tried so many times."

We talked for over an hour. We shared laughter, expressed joy, exchanged thoughts, and spoke of our mutual hope for a winter visit. And when we were satisfied we'd said all that we had to say, we hung up with promises to call one another again—soon.

The scripture says that God "knows the secrets of the heart" (Ps. 44:21, NIV). It also says, "All my longings lie open before" Him, and "my sighing is not hidden from" Him (38:9, NIV).

I've experienced those times when I haven't known how I ought to pray. I will, no doubt, know such moments again. But how wonderful to know Rom. 8:26 is a promise we can stand on—even long-distance. How wonderful to know "the Spirit himself intercedes for us with groans that words cannot express" (NIV).

Wisdom

My daughter and I had driven just half a block from church when I turned, glanced out my side window, and spotted a fellow worshiper with a cigarette hanging from his lip.

"Look at that!" I blurted. "Comes straight out of church and already lighting up." I grunted an audible, self-righteous, "Humpf."

For several seconds, Lisa was silent. Then, softly, she spoke. "Look at that. Comes straight out of church and already judging."

All About Hedges and Growing Up

When my husband is out of town, my waking up once or twice a night isn't unusual. I'm not afraid; I just don't sleep as well in our oversized bed without my spouse. But one night, I didn't wake up just once or just twice; I woke up four times. And each time my eyes opened, my youngest daughter came to mind.

"Pray a hedge of protection around Lisa," I seemed to hear every single time I tossed and checked the clock.

A former pastor had frequently spoken of hedges and protection and prayer. He'd often advised parents to pray daily hedges around our kids.

At first, I wasn't so sure I believed it was all that necessary. But because the teaching had impressed my husband, we soon began joining hands and praying hedges every morning before Scotty left for work. This week, however, with my spouse away on business, I'd prayed the hedges alone. And last night, each time I tugged blankets up around my neck and buried my head in my pillows, I whispered, "Father, I pray a hedge of protection around Lisa, again, in the name of the Lord Jesus Christ."

The first prayer was offered around 11 P.M., EST. In Seattle, where our daughter is a senior at the University of Washington, it was 8 P.M.

I was awakened again at midnight, one o'clock, and if I remember correctly, sometime around 3:30 or 4 A.M. I can't pin the last time down, because I was worn out with waking up.

By 5 A.M. when my alarm sounded, I felt thoroughly wrung out, and I'd completely forgotten about hedges and protection. Not until the telephone rang and I heard my daughter crying at the other end of the line did I remember my prayers.

"Mom," Lisa sobbed. "Oh, Mom. Last night," she said, crying still, "I heard this noise in my apartment."

My face froze, my legs seemed to lose it, I dropped into a chair and glanced at the kitchen clock: 7:30 A.M. in Washington.

"*What* noise? When? Where—?"

"A rat!" Lisa shrieked. "And it wouldn't leave and it kept running and scratching across the linoleum . . ."

Earlier, Lisa had nonchalantly mentioned cockroaches. She'd also casually announced that four nights in a row someone had broken into her car. Packages I'd mailed her had been stolen from outside her apartment door.

My husband and I hadn't been surprised by any of these revelations. The first time we'd flown to the West Coast to see her "cutest apartment," we'd both come away wondering if we shouldn't just tie her up and take her home.

"Oh, Honey." I pinched my jaw between my cold fingers, trying not to cry along with my youngest child. "How long has this been going on?" I asked, my voice infirm and my temples throbbing so that I could barely hear myself speak.

Lisa's tears finally under control, she said she'd been having trouble for several nights. Something had been getting into her wastebaskets and plants and some of her food. She'd suspected a mouse. But last night she'd flipped on an overhead light and discovered the rat. Longer than the palm of her hand, she said, and its tail even longer than that.

"You could have been bitten!" Did she call the landlord? I wanted to know.

"No," Lisa peeped. She'd phoned a friend who'd insisted she get out of the apartment as fast as she could. And she'd fled. In the middle of the night. Down dimly lit streets where sidewalks buckle, toward her car, which may or may not have been tampered with. Through a neighborhood where muggings and break-ins are current events. Wearing a short nightgown and robe.

"You could have been grabbed!" I whooped.

"Mom, I didn't know what else to do." She was crying again.

Would I have known what else to do? I wondered. Probably not. I'm like gelatin when it comes to cockroaches, car thieves, and rats.

So we talked and decided on a plan. She would call her landlord, tell him he was to meet her at her apartment door and go in with her while she packed a bag. She was giving notice. She wouldn't live with rats. She would request that her damage deposit and her final month's rent be returned. She would find other housing. Something clean. An apartment large enough for roommates, protected parking, a security system or guard.

After 25 minutes on the phone, Lisa seemed settled and satisfied.

"But, Lord," I prayed, "*I* feel frustrated. I want to fly right out there, rent a U-haul, throw out all of Lisa's perishables, gather and scrub the rest of her belongings, and *bring her home!*"

Still, I knew if he were here what my husband would say. He'd tell me Lisa was no longer a child; she was a young woman, an adult.

Tapping out my frustration on the table's top, I admitted that I knew not only what Scotty would say but also what Lisa wanted. She wanted to graduate in December, to become established in a line of work for which she's become more than qualified, to become a mature woman—one able to deal with life *without* her mother's holding her hand.

"So, what am I to do?" I breathed as I placed the receiver back into its cradle and walked away from the phone, hoping God had listened in.

"Pray a hedge of protection," the suggestion came again.

"That's it?" I protested, at a pitch that couldn't exactly be called prayer.

It worked last night, didn't it?

Well, yes, I had prayed, and my daughter had been protected as she'd sprinted through darkened alleys above the freeway, surrounded by broken street lamps and heaven only knows what else! She had

63

made it to her friend's, hadn't she? And, now that we'd talked and she'd thought things out, she did seem ready to do what had to be done.

"OK, Father," I said, at first reluctantly and then with my strong will restrained. "I'll pray the hedge."

I spotted Lisa's grin in a picture in the hall.

"And then," I said, nodding, "I'll entrust *Your* daughter to *You*. But," I added, "now that You've taught me about hedges, do You suppose You might speed up Lisa's growing up and mine too? At my age, I don't think I can handle many more long-distance revelations or sleepless nights—hedges or no."

Try God

Two bookmarks arrived in my afternoon mail. On each were the words "Try God." Scanning the accompanying letter, I walked to my sewing room, the Bible lying on my desk, and God's still, small voice: "Put them into your book bag and take them to school tomorrow."

Too often the skeptic, I thought, That makes no sense. I don't need them there. I need them here, in my Bible.

But again I seemed to hear, "Be still, and know that I am God" (Ps. 46:10, KJV).

So I turned, walked to my work area, and laid both bookmarks beside my canvas bag.

The next day, the markers packed in the bag but forgotten, I drove to work as usual and began the day with third period, as usual. As usual, I also threatened my seniors to be silent for the school district's mandated silent sustained reading. Then, because they were particularly restless, I followed the clock for the entire 20-minute reading period, anxious to be rid of the entire bunch!

This class had given me trouble like no other. I prayed over them, cried over them, and even threatened to resign over them! Some were sullen, sluggish 20-year-olds who read at the sixth grade level and fought learning anything new. Some were drug dealers, boys who'd been in the Detention Center for "minor" crimes, and angry girls who solicited attention without remorse.

I had great difficulty seeing any of them as God did, and I longed for the year's end.

This particular morning when the bell finally shrieked, almost everyone bolted from the room, and I had turned to the chalkboard when one boy hesitated at my desk.

"Mrs. H., do you by any chance have a bookmark?"

I was flabbergasted! The year was nearly over. They'd read every day. No one had asked for a bookmark before. But here stood a boy who'd talked with me several times. His mom was a Christian; his dad was not. He often drove his mother to church because it pleased her, but he dreaded having to attend. He'd tried church, tried drugs, tried transcendental meditation, and was now into something new: a combination of the spiritual and the martial arts.

"Yes," I said, "I do." I fumbled through my bag until I found one of the wheat-colored markers. He looked down at it, looked up, half smiled, and left.

Still amazed over the request, I turned again to the chalkboard—and heard the heavy, cleated boots of a second boy. One who had started out the door but was now on his way to my desk.

"Mrs. Hoag, ya gotta bookmark on ya?"

My mouth dropped open. "Why, yes. I just happen to have one." Again, I dug through the bag, located the marker, offered it, and watched the boy's face as he looked it over.

"Humpf," he muttered. "Thanks." And out the door he went, nodding, grinning back over his shoulder. He was on his way, I was certain, to get stoned. He was into drugs in a big way. In fact, he was joining the military because he'd heard drugs were easier to get there. We'd talked once in a while about the Lord. He thought it was fine for an "older person" like me. He sometimes wrote poetry about God. But his "god" was somehow a part of his drugs.

As the second boy's back passed through the doorway, I dropped to my chair. "Lord, I only have two bookmarks; what if someone else comes?" But the entire day passed, and no one did. The week passed, and no one did. And finally, the last day of school came without one request for another marker.

Other requests came, however. Requests that made me know how hungry my students were and that taught me, also, just how anxious God is to feed them.

I remember one day knowing one of my students was in trouble. The Lord seemed to draw her to my attention. She needed someone.

So I watched for a time to share the Lord with her. The time came one day when she didn't show up for class.

I found her in the main hall: red-eyed and headed out the front door. At first she was reluctant, but by the time we finished talking, she'd smiled and we'd prayed. She recommitted her life to the Lord, redecided to trust Him. And at the end of the year, I had a new plaque over my desk, a gift from a once-starved child who'd experienced the Lord's renewing. The plaque read, "You have touched me; I have grown."

Then there was Scott, a scruffy, foul-behaved kid. I'd begged the Lord to get him out of my class! But that same still, small voice said, "I want you to pray for him."

"I'll pray for him, all right," I murmured. "I'll pray for him to get out of my class!"

Still, at the Lord's urging, I found myself telling friends about him, kneeling at our church altar for him while at the same time contemplating approaching the school board about him. Until, one afternoon, when Scott walked into the library where I sat making out grades.

He'd been absent from my class for days. I was ready to snap at him until I looked into his face. What I saw I'll never forget: hollow eyes, dark circles, uncombed hair, unwashed hands, and clothes that were a disaster.

I retreated into my grade book to squeeze back tears. Drugs had all but eaten up Scott's youth.

As my student began to talk, he told me of a week of torment, days of trips, and how he'd finally had it and slashed his wrists.

As he pulled his sleeves up, I told him about the Lord. And that afternoon, Scott and I made a pact: If he would come to class each day and *try* to learn, I would pass him at the end of the year. Soon he was showing up for class: scrubbed, combed, smiling. And I discovered he was really so bright. At the end of the year, he'd passed English on his own.

Lost kids? Unloved? Unlovable? Then why did God urge me to help them and also provide the opportunities?

My students with those bookmarks in their possession? I don't know that I'll ever hear how the one is doing in the military, and I probably won't see the other boy again. But that incident on an April morning—and the others I've shared—marked an important lesson for me: He knows where each of those students are. Furthermore, to

66

me those kids might have seemed like "the pits," but He loves them and understands their confusion. And all that He requires of us is attentiveness to His whispered directives so that, one day, they will also hear His call and try God.

The Key

The cloudy skies over the Pacific Northwest matched the mood that haunted my oldest child's wedding. Fearing a confrontation between first and second spouses, tension had filled the air. My husband and I hardly slept the entire week.

Now we were to fly to Montana for another family gathering, long overdue and bound to be taxing. We were out of our hotel bed before dawn and still groggy. We had to force ourselves into action, since we had less than an hour to catch our flight.

"We'll make it," my husband said, wrapping his tired arms around me. "And, once these three weeks are behind us, we'll be glad we made the effort, Babe."

Truth was, neither my spouse nor I felt all that optimistic. After seven days of tension and occasional despair, we were both weary. Two more hectic weeks seemed almost more than either one of us could face.

We dragged three pieces of luggage down the dimly lit hall to the elevator and agreed: "It sure would be good to steal away for a time-out."

The lobby was empty. But with going-to-work traffic beginning to trumpet on the freeway below, we checked out, seized our bags, and carefully tucked each piece of luggage and souvenir into the rented car's trunk. My husband slammed the lid and let out one long groan.

"The key!" He'd locked it in the trunk. We had no spare.

He dashed for the phone, the rental car number clutched in his hand. But the agency told him, "Sorry, we're shorthanded this morning, and we don't have a runner we can send out. There's nothing we can do."

Taxi drivers who'd parked nearby offered help. One athletic cabby huffed and puffed, but the backseat wouldn't budge. A female driver picked the lock, but the trunk lid still wouldn't lift.

Weeping, I telephoned my youngest.

She suggested I was just tired. "You know how you are, Mom." She asked if I'd prayed. Then she hung up.

I mumbled a quick, impassioned prayer (plea bargaining) and ran back to the car.

Meanwhile, Yellow Pages tucked under his arm, a bellboy suggested a locksmith. Why hadn't we thought of that?

My husband hurried to the nearest phone: Would the specialist come *now?*

"Yes," he said. He'd be there "with time to spare." However, more than an hour passed before he showed his face, 30 minutes *after* our flight had departed and with a bill nearly double the original quote.

We decided there was nothing we could do but pay the fee and call the airline to explain why we'd been delayed.

"It will cost an additional $600 to rebook your flight," a male voice said.

"We don't have $600," I declared, trying to sound more composed than I felt.

"Come in and we'll talk about it, but you'll have to get here *soon*," the man said. He pronounced his name and spelled it for me.

Halfway to the airport and at a speed just a tad beyond the law, we discovered we were lost. We circled south, then north.

I bowed my head and appealed again. But we arrived even later than I'd predicted on the phone.

"Oh, Scotty . . . now what?"

"It'll work out, Babe," my husband consoled me. "Just don't worry. OK? I know you're tired, but take my hand and we'll pray. Then I'm going to drop you off at the entrance. You get into line with the luggage. I'll get rid of the car and meet you before you ever get up to the desk."

I eyed the stern-looking agent at the ticket window and measured the distance between myself and the man. What if my husband didn't get back to me in time? Still, the line was nearly 30 persons long.

Again I petitioned. I'd no sooner relaxed, however, when my number came up, and Scotty hadn't shown up. And I quit praying and cried.

I couldn't speak. I didn't know where I'd hidden our tickets. And I hadn't written down the name of the man who'd told us, "Come in and talk."

For more than a minute I seized great gulps of air and wailed while the poor, uniformed agent looked as if he wished I'd go away.

Finally I ran out of tears.

The ticket agent looked relieved.

I opened my mouth to explain why we'd missed our plane and why we'd taken longer getting to the airport than we'd planned, and the reservations clerk found his voice.

"Everything's going to be OK," he said, as if he spoke to a toddler with two skinned knees. "I'll just talk to my super, and I'll be right back." Before I could say a word, he closed the window and nearly ran for the door.

I didn't wait long. Within seconds, the agent returned, fresh tickets in his hand. We were all set, at no extra charge.

I exited the line, spotted my husband, and laughingly exclaimed that I'd "taken care of the whole thing."

"Maybe so. But do you understand," Scotty asked, as we made our way through the crowd to a place where we could sit, "we'll have to lay over for more than half a day in Salt Lake? I'll have to call Mom and tell her we're going to be very late."

I did and I did not understand. Yes, I heard the man say we'd be laying over awhile, but what I didn't yet comprehend was that the Lord had answered prayer.

"Well, if we have to lay over, we have to lay over," I said, sighing. And within minutes we boarded our new flight.

"What'll we do for nearly a day?" I asked, once we'd fastened our seat belts.

"I don't know, Babe. Guess we can share my book."

Oh, terrific, I thought. Just what I wanted to read: a computer programming guide.

But we'd no sooner landed when a woman approached with, "I'm with Travel Aid. Can I give you an assist?"

"Well," I said, "I don't suppose you could get us to Montana in time for lunch."

She smiled. "I can't do that. But do you see those double doors up ahead?"

We did.

"If you hurry, you can just make the bus, and for 50 cents, you can get to town, grab a cable car, and eat lunch in Trolley Square."

"Trolley Square!" I exclaimed. We'd eaten lunch there once before—on the first day of our honeymoon.

It took no discussion. For weeks, Scotty and I had given little or no attention to ourselves or one another. We were supposedly on vacation, but we had not been refreshed. So, while the smiling woman watched, my spouse and I hugged, grabbed each other's hands, and ran. And for the rest of the day, we played.

After the trolley ride, we delighted in a Mexican lunch, something we'd longed for since our move from Albuquerque to the East. We even discovered our waitress hailed from my husband's hometown, and before long, she joined us for nostalgic asides.

Unlike the weather we'd experienced on the West Coast, the sun was warm and reassuring. We walked, talked, bought ice creams from a sidewalk stand, and dined on a park bench.

Later, as we buckled up for a sunset landing, we delighted in the thought that because of the accidentally locked trunk, we'd been treated to one blessed and restful afternoon to regroup, prepare for a second week of commotion, and encourage each other.

As we touched down and prepared to disembark, we understood we had planned the reunions and the fast-paced trip, but God had arranged for the rest. All along, He had held the key.

Puzzled Pieces, Rightly Fitted

Thoroughly discouraged, I'd done it again. In my eagerness to serve God, I'd shown up at all the wrong places, had become involved, volunteered without seeking God's direction, and had been forced to back out.

I was certain I should play the piano for our Christian women, but the day before what was to be my first performance, I suddenly sensed I was in deep water alone, out of His will completely.

Some weeks later, I felt called to teach the women's Bible study. I randomly gathered and tossed materials, women were recruited, fliers were mailed, I moved into a leadership role, and, even before the long hour ended, I realized I was again walking in ill-fitting shoes.

Back home, I wept. Where did He want me to serve? Surely there was a ministry for me. Many times I'd read, "But now hath God set the members every one of them in the body, as it hath pleased him" (1 Cor. 12:18, KJV).

Later that week, I shared with several close friends who prayed with me and promised they would continue to pray until the answer came. Meanwhile, they sent me Scripture verses, magazine clippings, and teaching pamphlets. Each confirmed there definitely was a place for me to serve. However, because I'm sometimes impatient, I found little comfort in any of it.

Finally, I went to the Lord determined to keep my lips sealed and my heart and ears open. (I wonder why it so often comes to "finally." Why do some of us wait until all else fails before we go to God on our knees and stay put until the answer comes?)

I hadn't spent many minutes in prayer before a picture began forming in my mind—a glimpse of a jigsaw puzzle composed of, perhaps, a thousand pieces. Two of those pieces were nearly identical. That is, their shapes were so similar they could have easily fitted into either of two empty spaces, unless you'd seen the entire picture beforehand or, better yet, created the puzzle yourself.

Suddenly I realized how easily a barn piece might end up in the middle of a New England wood, or a fragment of blue sky might stand out awkwardly in the side of an otherwise red barn.

Thoughts began to surface that could only have originated with God. "I've created you for a particular spot. Where do you feel you fit? Are you sky? Barn?" Then He opened my spiritual eyes, and I knew there was one place where I always felt at home, absolutely snug. At my typewriter in the spare bedroom we'd renamed "Nancy's Office." That was where I belonged, with a pot roast simmering in the kitchen, sheets drying on the backyard lines, and a cookie jar filled to overflowing for my family.

As I stood and glanced out my window, the leaning barn across the street caught my eye. The sight of it encouraged me to write several articles. Overhead, a flock of Canadian geese were silhouetted against azure blue, and I knew I would, one day soon, describe them for a reader, as well. And, on the lawn, squirrels headed for the feeder and corn they counted on me to supply.

"Yes, I fit here just fine," I said.

There is a woman who is to be the Bible teacher. She'll come forward soon. And someone else is to play the piano. She's probably running through limbering-up exercises right now. And me? I'm feeling settled in, nicely limited and fitted into the Body. And, along with the other members, I can just imagine we present a pleasing picture before our Maker.

71

Prodigal's Play

Relaxing in our Datsun while my husband shopped for some tool he needed, I vaguely regarded assorted people scurrying in and out of stores, darting across parking lots against brisk winds, lumbering along with small children in tow. I was, however, disinterested until my attention was arrested by a young father, a child who appeared to be five or six, and a toddler dressed in pink ruffles and ebony curls caught up in a matching barrette.

As the threesome approached the entrance of an ice cream and candy parlor, the older child obviously understood what was in store. Without hesitation, she charged through the shining glass entry where piñatas, candy-striped chairs, and glass jars filled with assorted confections beckoned customers from the other side of the enormous plate glass window. Even I began to wonder if a trip home without ice cream was a possibility.

It soon appeared, however, the younger child was totally unimpressed. That she was at last free from the infant's car seat and out of her father's hand seemed uppermost in her mind. She squealed delightedly, toddled onto the sidewalk, and headed in exactly the opposite direction from which the call came.

Meanwhile the older sister stepped to the counter inside the store. The father stopped just short of entering. And I became totally absorbed by the minidrama, wondering who would come out the winner in what was shaping up to be a battle of the wills.

Stepping back from the door, the father watched as his child began running on short legs, threw her arms into the air, and reeled toward the store next door.

When she'd traveled several yards, her father called her name.

She did not respond.

He called again.

Slowly she turned, the grin on her face seeming to say, "I'm deciding. Maybe I'll come. Maybe I won't."

Again the father called, and the child took several steps toward outstretched arms, then suddenly stopped. For a second or two she

72

swayed, unsure of her legs, yet obviously enjoying even an uncertain freedom. About the time it seemed the father might be winning, the child threw her arms into the air and pressed dimpled hands to her flushed cheeks.

Once again her father called, and this time he stepped toward his daughter and smiled.

The child's response was a delighted whoop! That her overseer was making such an effort to draw her to himself seemed to please her. However, instead of resounding with open arms and obedience, she spun on one unsteady foot, kicked out a pink corduroy-covered leg, and dashed on tiptoe for the store next door.

Just before she reached the push-bar, a merry-go-round caught her eye. She stopped, tipped her head as if she were considering it as an alternate plan, and turned slightly as the father petitioned once more.

Again she did not respond. But this time, instead of approaching the child, the father turned as if he'd given up and edged toward his original destination. While the young father casually walked away, I watched the child.

She looked as if she was considering both his invitation and his apparent retreat while, at the same time, determining to make up her *own* mind in her *own* time.

Why would this child choose to wander first from one distraction and then to another?

In the middle of my question my Heavenly Father gave me an answer, one which applied not only to a tiny child but to me, one of His older children, as well.

How many times in my walk had I heard His call, and how often had I deliberated, deciding whether to respond or run?

On numerous occasions He'd not only called me by name but also stretched out His arms, inviting me to share in a better joy. But I'd become distracted, not simply by outside attractions but by my own desires and willfulness.

"Father," I whispered; but as I did so, the child's laughter captured me once again.

Her grin was comic and her manner coquettish as she tipped her head and studied her father's face.

Once more arms were extended to the child as the unruffled parent smiled and continued his patient appeal.

For several seconds it appeared the playful tot had no intention of obeying, and I expected the young father would be forced to take three giant steps, grab his offspring, and drag her into the store. However, suddenly and with the same enthusiasm she'd displayed as a runaway, the toddler tossed round arms upward, shrieked happily, and raced toward her parent—where she was met with a hug, a twirl up into the air, and a bounce and hop across the walk and into the confectioner's shop.

Returning to my private thoughts and wandering, I considered the occasions when I'd wondered if my way might be the better way, or at the very least, the most exciting course. But my Father had also waited patiently, had also smiled on me. My Father had also extended himself even as I'd considered disobedience. And when I'd belatedly returned to Him, He'd lifted me back into that place where, in His presence and in His will, I had become joy filled. Where I'd discovered that abiding in Him surpasses prodigal's play.

More than One Teacher in the Classroom

Since early fall I'd petitioned for help with my students labeled "dopers" by the community. Eighteen and 19, they read at the fourth-grade level, consumed drugs, and were not only challenging but often combative! As a result, I spent hours on my praying toes. Occasionally, I set English studies aside and explained my earlier training as a drug education teacher. I also shared the Lord. No one seemed to hear my words on *either* subject. Consequently by the end of most days, I sat at my desk with my head in my hands and my mind on retiring.

After several months, I was near to giving up. Exhausted, I wondered if God expected me to battle alone, until one morning when Robert and Kristy joined our class.

Committed Christians, my new students became the brightest spot in my day, the first to arrive and always the last to leave. We exchanged prayer requests, even prayed together before the others arrived. Days when I'd decided to give up, they'd grin, encourage with "Hang in there, Mrs. H.," and remind me they were praying too. During S.S.R. (a mandated silent sustained reading program) they read their Bibles and tracts. When the others heckled, Robert and Kristy offered to share their reading material, then smiled at the jokes and taunts.

Daily, as I witnessed the gentle testimonies, my faith began to grow, and I began reading my Bible openly without fear of ridicule *or* the administration. The other students craned necks, elbowed one another, and just above a whisper, offered snide remarks while I prayed seeds planted would one day take root.

Then one morning I dashed through my kitchen, gathering books and magazines for the reading table. Weekly, I'd imported material from home, hoping at least one student might discover reading. On my way to the car, arms full, I spotted a Christian publication. The feature article was "How I Kicked the Habit: Marijuana." The boy on the cover resembled many of my students. I vowed to read the article as soon as I returned home. However, I hadn't reached the garage before I was back in the kitchen and grabbing the periodical almost as a response to a command.

"That couldn't have been the Lord. My family hasn't even read this one yet," I mumbled, entering the parking area and heading for my portable.

In the first hour, several students milled around the book table, rifled through, glanced at, and "borrowed" just one magazine: the Christian periodical.

I was shocked. From the beginning of the year we'd had an understanding: I'd provide reading material, but it wasn't to leave the room. And although students had given me trouble about nearly everything else, the one rule they'd abided by was the one about the reading table. Until now.

"Lord," I prayed, "please touch the heart of that student who, this very minute, has something in his hands that's capable of turning his life around. Help him, Father, I pray." Then I remembered my encouragers.

Everyone had bolted for the door at the first bell except for Robert and Kristy, who were discussing the fellowship they'd attended the night before. I told them about the mission magazine. They rejoiced, and we prayed, claiming a student for Christ. Then they exited the room while I considered the stark contrast between the two who knew Him and those who did not.

The school year passed. I supplied more magazines and books, even comics. But nothing left the room.

In June, as I prepared to close up for the summer, I thought back to those times when one boy and then another had lingered around my desk, attempting nonchalance and pretending disinterest in the things of God. But there had been questions. They'd asked if I were a Christian. They'd asked if I really believed Jesus was the Son of God. Was He really coming again? Did I believe "all that heaven-and-hell stuff"?

I'd done my best to meet their queries with answers from God's Word. But when Kristy and Robert were nearby, I'd also referred the questioners to them.

I never discovered which student had the magazine, but I did see God's stirring in at least six lives. One boy began bringing *his* Bible, though he was reticent to talk. A number of boys became friends with Robert, and I overheard him invite them all to his church. Another began talking to his father about the Lord. And a girl, hardened by a life that had stolen her youth, gave me a chain on the last day of the year. On it was a key and the words: "He set me free." Then, though she refused to talk, she returned my hug with a warmth I'd never suspected she possessed. One boy came to say good-bye with eyes cast down and suggesting, as he shuffled his boots back and forth, that we "just might be right about a few things." This boy, during the course of the year, had cleaned himself up, improved in his studies, and smiled. And I was reminded that not only does our Father know when sparrows fall, but also He'd known when our classroom door opened and closed.

As I walked toward my car and summer vacation, I thought of my two special students, and I thanked God that there'd been more than one teacher in the classroom that year.

The Art of Putting Off Prayer

"In the morning, O Lord, Thou wilt hear my voice; in the morning I will order my prayer to Thee and eagerly watch" (Ps. 5:3, NASB).

I don't know what I thought was so important that first morning, the day I decided to skip devotions and get to work instead.

On the second day, I mentally listed excuses, reasons for putting my Bible aside again. "But," I promised, "I'll read and pray and study later."

By the third day, it was quite easy. No excuses offered, silently or otherwise. No promises made. I simply didn't pray. I had much on my mind now, with holidays creeping up on my calendar, and my children soon flying home. Besides, the weekend was coming: I'd spend a long afternoon, instead of the usual 30 minutes first thing each day. The Lord would understand.

However, the weekend came, and it was even busier than I'd anticipated. First, Saturday began with breakfast out. And then, since we were already on the road, my husband suggested we deal with errands and shop for gifts. Noon came and we were hungry, so we ate lunch on the run as well. Back home, we discovered it was nearly time to dress: We'd made dinner plans with friends.

"Tomorrow, Lord," I whispered, getting ready for my shower and laying out a fresh suit.

Tomorrow came, but my quiet time did not. Yes, I went to church, listened to the pastor, and prayed along. But time with the Lord? Alone? I never found a minute I thought I could spare.

Meanwhile, my work began to feel like an unpleasant chore. All over my desk, I had article ideas on scraps of paper. And there were deadlines to meet. But instead of turning to the Lord—spending time before Him and requesting His aid—I told myself, "If I just pop into my office earlier each morning and return to work after dinner, I'll catch up."

But Christmas arrived, and so did my children, and I hadn't caught up. Hadn't even come close.

By New Year's Day, a day I normally find special, a day when I usually feel I'm off and flying with a brand-new fresh start, my goals seemed too far beyond me. I lamented loudly, certain every other writer was beginning to realize success. Everyone but me. I began to fear the lonely days with the house empty again, wondering if, maybe, I'd look for "real work."

"I'll never make it," I told my spouse. "At my age, why even try?"

And it wasn't just my writing world that seemed to be falling apart. Pennsylvania winters were beginning to get on my nerves. A friend began calling daily, and I began to dread the sound of her voice. It looked as if my husband would be transferred to a place I felt I couldn't bear. At first, I wept. Later, I raved. Then, one morning—in my office but unable to work—I finally dropped to my knees.

"Lord, why am I in the pits?"

I found His answer in my prayer journal when I opened it and discovered five weeks worth of blank sheets.

They say a journey begins with a single step. That's exactly how mine began. I had meant only to postpone one morning's quiet time, but that particular day I never became quiet at all. The second and third days I made the same excuses and promised I'd get back on track soon. But for more than a *month,* I hadn't spent one tranquil *minute* before the Lord. And it showed.

"Lord," I whispered, "forgive me. I can't manage on my own. I need this time with You, need You to quiet me, need You to direct my thoughts. I can't do my work without You; *You* are the reason for my work."

Within minutes, peace came and calm. I sensed a new set of directions. I settled back into my chair and began to type.

But peace, calm, and flowing words were not the only indications the Lord had forgiven and renewed. That morning I received calls from no less than two editors, one to offer an extraordinary assignment, the other to save me from embarrassment.

This morning I praise God for teaching me some things during these past several weeks: I may choose to teach, bake wedding cakes, or write. I may prefer to relocate or elect to stay put. But my quiet time can never become a matter of choice. I must begin each day listening and in prayer. Then He will direct my paths, and joy will come anew.

PART 3

FOR RAINY DAYS

"He will be like rain falling on a mown field, like showers watering the earth."

Ps. 72:6, NIV

Even in Deepest Waters

Bent on divorce, her husband was leaving, and my friend flailed her arms in despair as I sought the Lord for words I might speak, some way I might console.

"I can't keep my head above water," Linda wept.

As she spoke, my thoughts began to wander, a memory surfaced, and while Linda sat quiet, I began telling her about my children and the year all three were just learning to swim.

"At first, their teacher asked only that they place their mouths and noses to the water and make bubbles," I said. "Then they progressed to dunking, splashing, floating across the instructor's arms, and, one day, swimming the full length of the Olympic-sized pool.

"But one of my children had cried at the thought of the deeper waters from her first initiation into the wading end of the pool. She'd begged her teacher not to leave her; and then when it seemed her protests had been ignored, she'd thrown herself into *my* arms, clutching me as if she might never let go."

"And?"

"And, kneeling beside her and meeting her eye-to-eye, I whispered, 'Don't be afraid. Trust your teacher for one step at a time.' Shortly after, my offspring rested, finally convinced that when the time came, she would be able."

As my friend Linda became still and leaned back quietly from my kitchen table, I said, "You know, I just read a scripture the other day: 'He reached from on high, he took me, he drew me out of many waters'" (Ps. 18:16, RSV).

Linda didn't smile as if she hadn't a care in the world, but she did nod and quietly, but audibly, acknowledge renewed faith. God would lead her by His Spirit, even in the depths. She would not sink.

A Lapful of Lilacs

It seemed to me I needed a miracle.

Dressing for work, my mind was in a whirl, reviewing all the problems facing me: none of them major—just an accumulation of minor irritations.

I was teaching at a small, struggling, Christian high school, where teachers not only taught but also served lunch, cleaned bathrooms, and directed "inspirational" chapel services.

My husband, whose work had taken him to Texas, Nebraska, and Nigeria, was away on another trip. The night he had left, our car had broken down at a shopping center, several miles from home. A friend had towed it back to our drive. But there it sat, waiting for my spouse's return.

Now, as I raced down the street in my husband's beat-up truck, the problems seemed to pass in review: the mutinous car, finding time to take my daughter to one instructor tonight, her voice lesson tomorrow, and the orthodontist who would only see my child during *my* working hours.

It was also that time teachers dread: semester's end and time for grades. Time to decide: Do I give him the grade he earned and risk an hour with his upset mom? Or should I fudge a little in his favor, hoping he'll be encouraged and do better, but really knowing my conscience will keep me on edge for a week?

Furthermore, our dog-pound dog—an accomplished escape artist—had tunneled under the iron gate and seemed to be daring everyone on the street to call the animal shelter. Our cat was spending his mornings in the neighbor's bird feeder, eating buttered toast while waiting for the main course to fly in. And my husband wouldn't be home for days.

It seemed to me it would take a miracle to help me juggle appointments, school grades, pets, and a temperamental pickup truck until Scotty's return.

The school building was almost in sight when I rolled down the windows of the cab to let in some fresh, morning air and caught the scent of lilacs: the Spokane flower. Spokane, Wash., where I'd grown up climbing trees, running through the pine woods with my best dog, Pal. Where I'd vowed never to love anyone but Mike Nichols—even after sixth grade and even though my family moved me clear across the state.

Lilacs. In Spokane, they had grown wild in our yard. They'd flourished at Grandma's too. Purple or white, they were beautiful. Lilacs were spring. Lilacs were childhood play days. And now, lilacs bloomed everywhere in Albuquerque, everywhere but our place, that is. We had moved to New Mexico the year before but had spent the planting season unpacking boxes, painting bathrooms, and dog-proofing the backyard. So we hadn't planted a thing.

Now, as I gulped great breaths of lilac-scented air, I prayed aloud, "Father, how I would love to have an armload of those flowers right now! Enough of them to bury my face in, enough to fill my lap!" I even confessed a longing to stop the truck, to stretch across a stranger's fence, and to pick a bunch. But I resisted and drove on.

Pulling into my spot in the school parking lot, I grabbed my books, slid out of the driver's seat, whispered another quick prayer—this one about the taxing day ahead—and dashed through the double metal doors right into a tall, gangly boy named Kit.

Shy and quiet, he wasn't one of the usual "greeters" who'd been following me to the classroom morning after morning with the hope of prying out of me what a grade would be.

"Good morning, Mrs. H.," he said.

"Good morning, Kit," I replied hastily as I hunched over the load of textbooks, stood first on one foot and then the other, and tried to pass by his lanky frame.

He smiled timidly. "I brought you something. It's in the kitchen."

Books crammed under my chin, the strap of my shoulder bag dangling at my elbow, I mumbled a "thank you," struggled down the poorly lit hall, dumped books onto my desk, and made my way to the kitchen for a *large* cup of black coffee.

"Father, give me strength," I moaned as I shoved the door open—and stopped dead still.

A strong fragrance engulfed me, not of freshly brewed coffee and not from yesterday's unattended garbage pail. It was lilac. On the counter, there was an enormous white and purple bouquet with a note: "Dear Mrs. H., have a good day."

I dropped into a kitchen chair, flowers in my lap, and pressed my nose right into the center of my surprise. I laughed. I cried. And I thanked my Heavenly Father. I thanked Him for lilacs. I thanked Him for the thoughtfulness of a young boy. And I thanked Him for loving me, for answering "small" prayers, and for sending "little" miracles.

My courage bolstered and my faith revived, I walked back to my classroom, my arms full of lilacs. And I knew that despite our troubled vehicle and our cat's perching where my neighbor begged him no, I'd just rest in my Father's love and there find sufficient strength to cope until my husband's return.

What Do You Expect of Me?

I tried liking her, but finally I had to admit it: Ruth got on my nerves. Every month at our church meeting she singled me out. Sometimes I managed to engage in conversation with a friend or bury my face in my notebook, hoping she'd take the hint.

It wasn't that I didn't understand she was a lonely sort, had difficulty making friends, and looked to me and the others for encouragement. "But," I'd moaned to my family over dinner, "I just don't have it. God didn't give me the gift of mercy or encouragement or *whatever* it takes to put up with *that girl!*"

For one thing, Ruth whined. I told myself that was the problem. I did not whine and couldn't tolerate people who did.

Then there was her chewing. "Father," I pleaded, "surely You expect us to have good manners! It's hard to bear, even for a Christian."

Driving to our monthly meeting, I pictured how I would once again avoid Ruth. As I walked into the room, I spotted her talking with a newcomer. She was reciting her now-familiar litany: how lonely she was, how no one understood, how she'd been "called" to minister but wasn't "getting the breaks."

Honestly! I fumed silently. Hope she doesn't drive a prospective member away! Then I scurried across the room, slid into a chair as far from her as possible, piled my coat and books into the empty seat beside me, and prayed "someone likable" would soon claim it. Ruth had selected a seat at the table in front of mine when our leader, Donna, nudged me and asked, "Say, Nancy, would you mind sitting up front? I have materials I want passed out, and I need you to make sure they get around."

I wanted to wail, "Oh, no, *please,* no." But as she transported my coat and books next to the one person I'd avoided for weeks, I gave up. I didn't want the others to find out I was less saintly than the radiant smile on my face indicated.

It went exactly as I'd anticipated—she talked incessantly! By the time the meeting got under way, I was so exhausted from listening I could hardly wait for dismissal. I thought seriously about never returning.

But the following month I did return, determined not to let anyone or anything make me miss the fellowship I so much enjoyed.

When Ruth stepped forward to greet me, I managed a plastic smile, sidestepped her, and struck up a conversation with Marilyn.

During the meeting, Ruth sat alone. She occasionally watched us laughing and cheering one another on good-naturedly, as close friends do. "But," I rationalized, "she isn't my problem. Lord, I just can't be responsible for everyone. Besides, we did try in the beginning to welcome her. Can I help it if she just doesn't fit in?"

After the meeting, she vanished, and I felt a small pang in my spirit. Immediately I shook it off as "not my concern," but just then our chairman tapped my shoulder.

"Hey!" she exclaimed. "All the prayer requests haven't been taken."

"I already have one," I said.

"Well," our chairman chided, rattling the lone request in the bottom of the basket, "we can't leave this one." Her eyes met mine. "Nancy, you're a good pray-er. You take it."

Before I could muster a protest, she dropped a wadded scrap of dirty paper into the palm of my hand; and the instant I saw it, I knew.

Outside in my car as I opened the tattered wad, my heart pounded, and my earlier question echoed inside my head: "Lord, what do You expect of me?" Then at the bottom of the slip I read the name: hers. Ruth asked for prayer because she wanted to become a writer, had never liked herself, and needed a friend.

My throat tightened and tears spilled. *I* understood the desire to write; it had been my heart's longing for years before I'd come up with sufficient courage to put pen to paper. Her low self-image? A Christian counselor had helped me with that too. And her last request? I could have been that friend.

"O God," I wept, "forgive me. I have sinned." I tried reminding myself that others felt as I did toward her, but there was no consolation. We'd all failed, and there was no comfort in that.

During the month, I spent much time on my knees. But the girl who'd grown heavy on my heart did not return. How much more pleasant it would be for me if she would only come back, I thought. At least, then, I might go through the motions and feel as if, somehow, I had redeemed myself. But instead, every time our group met, her absence reminded me of my shame—that I had not ministered to even "one of the least of these" (Matt. 25:40, 45, KJV).

Then one day, while I was attending a conference with my husband, she tapped me on the shoulder. When I turned to face her, I don't know who was more surprised. I grabbed that girl and hugged her as if she'd just returned from the grave. And, in truth, the smile on her face seemed to say she had.

We laughed and chattered until we were worn-out. She'd gone back to school. She'd made friends and found work. And the ministry she'd envisioned was becoming concrete. She was, at last, happy. And so was I.

That evening as I knelt before the Lord, I knew I owed Him thanks. Not only had He answered prayers for Ruth, but over the months He had begun to change my attitude too. A lonely girl had become joy-filled, and I, because God is patient, was becoming what He expected me to be—a woman with a servant's heart.

Planted, It Shall Bring Forth

I contemplated the near half-dozen gray squirrels, busy in our backyard since early morning, burying nuts and seeds.

Recalling the previous snow-covered winter, I imagined theirs was a survival plan. Come spring, each of these critters would return to underground pantries and make up for a long winter of meager provisions. However, that evening as I described my morning's activities and each varmint's antics, my husband chuckled.

"But don't you know?" He laughed. "Those squirrels seldom return to their larder. In fact, the reason unexpected crops sprout up in the middle of our garden *and* backyard is because those characters plant, then forget where or what they've hidden away!"

In that instant, I recalled burdens I'd entrusted with the Lord months ago. But I'd taken them back, returned them for a short period of time, and then, fretting, dug each one up again.

As I considered the squirrel's forgetfulness, I wondered if God wanted me to bury my concerns about my winter experiences with Him. Was I to become forgetful as well? If I did, would something good grow? Would God produce fruit perhaps where I least expected it in His way and in His own season?

In my heart, I knew His Word provided the answer. I had only to hide my fears in Him, and He would "make . . . grass to grow upon the mountains" (Ps. 147:8, KJV).

An Invitation to a Treasure Hunt

It was Friday. My husband would be taking me to lunch if I could get myself together and join him. But today I doubted even dining with the person I loved best could end the despair I'd wallowed in for two days—despondency that had surfaced soon after my Wednesday "debut."

The Young Mothers Club from church had called. Would I consider speaking? They were calling on older women to share. I'd only just celebrated my 40th, so I hardly felt "older." Still, I'd lingered over Titus 2:4 earlier that day. So, certain I was being led to minister to women, I said, "Yes!"

Four weeks later, however, standing before my audience, I stammered and rambled, certain I was disappointing every woman in that hall. Depression seemed to wrap itself around me like a villain's leaden cloak. I labored through closing fragments of my notes, mumbled several happy-homemaker tips, and moved to retreat.

Some women, out of kindness I suspected, suggested I sit and share one on one. But I knew if I didn't hurry to the parking lot, I'd burst into tears and exclaim, "I have no right to mingle with women like you. I'm a *divorcée*."

Two hours later, I sat staring out my bedroom window. Old, familiar guilt feelings overwhelmed me.

"Lord, I'm supposedly brand-new. So why do I feel so ugly about myself?" Instantly I broke into bitter sobs mixed with anger and disgust.

Nearly 48 hours later, I dressed and skulked out my back door, emerging from my refuge only because my daughter needed a ride to school.

Numb, I delivered Lisa, all the while intending to head right back to my spot behind closed doors. However, rounding the corner and nearing our hill, a sign caught my eye: Garage Sale.

The sale signs were always out on Fridays, but this one fascinated me. So I braked, wheeled up St. Mary's Drive, and discovered a garage overflowing with women and baby things.

Fidgeting with my keys, I thought, I should go home. This won't be my kind of sale. Still, I felt drawn. I slid from the driver's seat and marched to the garage, expecting to skim, smile, and return to quarantine.

Other than baby items, there were only lamps and notions. "Wasted my time and gas," I mumbled. Then I spotted the books.

French Cookery tempted, but when I stretched across the table toward it, I also spotted a paperback *Good News for Modern Man, Today's English Version*. I picked it up. We have two, I thought. Why buy another? Still, I couldn't put it down. It was only a quarter, I reasoned. I could give it away if I decided I didn't need it.

I walked to the card table, plunked down coins for the cookbook, a miniature lawn chair for a two-year-old friend, and the *Good News*.

Back home, cloistered again in my kitchen, I considered returning to my bed but poured myself a mug of strong-smelling, leftover coffee instead.

Digressing toward the sewing room, I glanced again at the books. Why had I bought that *Good News?* Pages were probably missing, or a toddler had crayoned its insides.

Agitated, I picked up the Bible and flipped to the first page, expecting support for my theory about its condition, but I discovered instructions: "See page 344." I felt as if I'd been invited to join a treasure hunt.

Locating page 344, I read, "Everyone has sinned." Tears were coming. Rom. 3:23 was underlined: "Everyone has sinned and is far away from God's saving presence" (all TEV). At the bottom: "Turn to page 350."

Racing to the assigned page, I read, "The penalty for sin." Six short words from Rom. 6:23 stood out: "For sin pays its wage—death." And at the bottom, "See page 498."

I rushed to read, "The penalty must be paid!" Also, Heb. 9:27 was underlined: "Everyone must die once, and after that be judged by God."

But for throbbing temples, I became absolutely still. It seemed God himself was trying to tell me something: "EVERYONE!" We were *all* guilty. We would *all* be judged by God.

Though I'd read the words before and a counselor had often recited them, I hadn't believed. Instead, I'd pretended there'd been no previous marriage and no divorce. I'd praised God for my joy in my present marriage and vowed to please Him with my present life. Why, then, did the past persist?

I glanced at the bottom of the page. The book's former owner had written, "Look up page 432." And soon I read, "Salvation is a free gift." Specifically, "It is by God's grace that you have been saved through faith. It is . . . God's gift" (Eph. 2:8).

I knew *that* already! It still didn't show me how to let go of the self-loathing and shame. It didn't tell me what I was compelled to reveal about my past, why I felt I'd lost my citizenship, how I was supposed to go on from here!

Anguish fixed my stare until I spotted the next set of directions: "Now see page 211."

When I'd located the final message, I pulled out a chair and sat down.

"The gift must be received," I read. The verse was: "Some . . . did receive him and believed in him; so he gave them the right to become God's children" (John 1:12).

It was such a simple answer: "The gift must be *received*." God *had* forgiven. He *did* love me. He *had* offered me a brand-new life in Christ. But I hadn't yet received Him.

Trembling, I stumbled to my sewing room and dropped to my knees. My Father had offered the Gift. It was mine for the asking *if* I truly desired it. And I did. And I told Him so.

Within seconds, I thanked and praised Him and began to experience His forgiveness. And on my knees rejoicing, I forgave myself as well. Then, after dressing quickly and with as much flare as I could manage in minutes, I hurried to savor lunch with my spouse. I didn't intend to miss a minute of it. I had good news to share.

Plunging into God's Will

A. B. Simpson wrote, "Abraham's faith reposed on God himself. He knew the God he was dealing with. It was a personal confidence in One whom he could utterly trust."

Reading these words, my mind drifted to an incident that had taken place years earlier when my children's "utter trust" in their father was tested.

Our daughter, even before entering kindergarten, became a swimmer. Her brother, younger by 16 months, swam too. They'd taken lessons at the YMCA together, learned nearly every stroke together, and swam every inch of the Olympic-sized pool together. Then, one day, the inseparable pair stood at the edge of a motel pool. Their father was in water nearly to his shoulders, as our children teetered, bright-eyed and fairly dancing with excitement—waiting for their daddy to call out their name.

"Come on. Jump into my arms," he encouraged as he stood, feet firmly planted in the pool's deeper end.

Squealing and giggling with both anticipation and apprehension, each pressed the other to go first. This went on for several minutes before Tammy suddenly flung her arms upward in complete abandon, pushed off from the tips of her toes, and flew into her daddy's arms, the summer water, and—as her laughter testified—absolute joy.

Father and daughter played for several minutes, then moved to the shallow end where our delighted child was deposited for safekeeping. Then my husband returned to our son, whose knees had begun to shake.

Our youngest tried to grin as he edged toward the rim; but as he neared the water, his lips began to quiver, and he jumped back. Then he moved forward. And back. Meanwhile, his father encouraged, even cheered him on. Offered hands that had, only minutes before, faithfully and gently received Tammy. But Rob, within seconds, decided he couldn't or wouldn't plunge into those waters or his father's arms.

Before long, there was one dejected boy in the chaise longue—his

91

shivering frame pressed firmly against the webbing, his face pinched into a frown that threatened to break out into full-blown wailing. And while he sat, his sister jumped in and out of the water, enjoying her time with her father, alone, because her brother hadn't had the faith to take flight.

As that picture returned to me after nearly 18 years, I prayed, "I'm like that with You, Father. I watch the others—called out and in the swim of glorious activity. Trusting. Adventuring. Prospering."

I moaned, realizing how often I'd believed He loved the others best—had given them greater gifts. "But You haven't, Father. It's simply that I've stood at the water's edge with my toes curled and stiffened by fear—afraid to believe that when You call and stretch out Your arms, it's OK to boldly dive in, to lean, and to allow myself to be carried to the other side.

Today I reminisce once more, and I recall not only my daughter's pleasure but her father's as well. The smile on his face expressed delight, because his daughter had trusted him.

"Father," I pray, "renew my faith and trust in You. Cause me to plunge myself into that to which You have called me, knowing You will not let me sink. Amen."

My Friend Mariana

My husband and I had flown to Yugoslavia with plans to ski. However, we'd barely settled into our hotel when we discovered the slopes were intermediate to expert. *I* needed bunny hills. By morning, rain, fog, and bitter wind began boiling in. Then my husband made his announcement: He'd ski with the men if I "didn't mind."

How could I mind? We'd planned for weeks, dipped into our savings, and flown halfway around the world to ski. "But, Father," I murmured, as my husband met "the guys," his hat snug and his grin wide, "I do wish I knew someone." There were other women in our tour group, but they were "real" skiers. Like the men, they were headed for slopes I couldn't imagine traversing.

Soon after my "prayer," while I slumped in a near-empty lounge, a tour guide rushed in exclaiming, "A bus goes to Sarajevo. You will enjoy going along?"

Would I? For just $3.00 and it would fill my entire day? It took me three minutes to grab my coat, stuff dinars into my purse, and skate to the bus. But as I slid into a metal seat, I still longed to meet someone, though I was beginning to sense the "longing" was not entirely my own but one planted by the Holy Spirit himself. What I didn't know was that my tour had been "prearranged" and that "someone" was making her way down the hotel steps.

I didn't spot her until the bus began pulling away.

"Wait!" she called. Long blonde hair whipped her face. A wool scarf dangled from the collar of her coat. She wore no makeup, but she was one of the most beautiful women I'd ever seen. Even as she favored one leg, she was regal.

The driver offered no assistance, but the woman smiled as if he had.

The 25-mile ride took nearly an hour, but we said little to one another. Occasionally the woman smiled, pointed out something of interest along the way, asked where I wanted to go. Her English was elegant, but as locals boarded the bus, her exchange with them told me she was, like the others, a Yugoslav.

In town, the woman smiled, pointed to where I'd exit and catch a return bus. She explained she'd injured her leg. She'd continue on to the hospital for help.

For the next hour-and-a-half, I pretended to shop while I wondered about the woman and experienced an odd sadness.

Into my second hour of browsing, I joined forces with another American, also shopping for nothing in particular.

We'd eaten cakes and tortes and were looking for a Coke when I saw her again. In a packed emporium with hordes of people passing by, she smiled, nodded, offered a reserved wave, and waited for us to catch up.

"How are you doing?" she asked, her tone schooled and her manner warm.

"Fine," I said, casually. But I nearly grabbed the woman and gave her a hug.

"Good," she said before she limped into the crowd.

I watched her for several seconds, spotted a bargain, moved toward the merchandise, then stopped midaisle.

"I know you'll think this is crazy," I blurted to my American ally, "but I have to go back and find her."

"Her, who?"

"A woman I met on the bus," I said, pushing toward the main aisle and scanning the crowd while my bewildered coshopper raced along behind.

"What?" The American frowned as if I were deranged.

"I have to find that woman!" I peered over the tops of fur hats and spotted her wandering as if she were the foreigner and lost.

It took me several seconds to reach her with a shout. But when she turned around and discovered us, she seemed relieved.

I told her we were thirsty. "Would you like to join us?" I asked.

She didn't hesitate. She was experiencing "a bit of pain" and needed to sit awhile. She knew of a local coffee shop but hadn't wanted to go in alone.

Meanwhile, the American decided to "grab a few more things." And I crossed the street toward a cup of Turkish coffee with my new friend.

"My name is Mariana," she said.

I introduced myself.

She was "on holiday." She'd been "quite ill." The doctors had prescribed play and rest with her little girl. Her husband hadn't come along. He'd been unable to leave his work.

We talked not only over coffee but all the way back to our hotel. And when we parted in the lobby, I nearly suggested we "talk some more." But, I thought, she wants to be with Yugoslavians.

Inside my room, however, I couldn't settle down. I had to know more. So I headed for the lobby, praying all the way, down every single stair.

Entering the lounge, I saw her. She smiled. She was glad I'd come. She also wanted to talk.

What we shared still amazes me. First, she said her illness was cancer; I'd had cancer. She'd survived a painful divorce; me too. She was an English teacher; so was I. She sang with a community choir; I sing. She'd remarried 10 years ago; Scotty and I had flown to Yugoslavia to celebrate our 10th. I told her I was a Christian; she responded with tears. She had been raised by a godly Christian mother. Mariana had once wholly believed. Trusted. Walked with God. But today she felt she'd been forsaken.

"Often I enter the sanctuary when it is empty, hoping to speak with God," she said. "Hoping to understand my disease."

I told Mariana every time I'd felt a "lump or bump" (for several years following two surgeries), I'd succumbed to fear until I discovered

God's peace, strength, and hope. I reminded her He was Healer and what the Bible says about faith.

Then I told her I'd "impulsively" tucked Christian magazines into my suitcase for "someone." Her face lit up.

I hurried to my room, located the periodicals, and spotted, for the first time, a cover article titled "Life After Cancer."

"O Father," was all I could manage as I raced downstairs.

That exchange opened the door to serious conversation and wonder-filled fun. I had no walking boots; Mariana gave me a pair of hers. We shared cakes, pizza, and our thoughts about faith. We captured snow pictures and found we both loved the outdoors. I shared America; Mariana told me about Dubrovnik and life by the sea. Would I come visit, meet her "dear husband" whom she "loved so much"?

I vowed I'd try, and we parted laughing, hugging, crying, and encouraging one another's faith.

I'd only been home two weeks when Mariana's letter arrived to say her world had fallen apart.

"This time it is quite serious." Although she'd previously undergone 14 months of chemotherapy, the cancer had surfaced again.

Curious about the black-bordered enclosure, I read on until my eyes fell on "the worst has happened in my life. My beloved husband has been murdered."

It couldn't be. I'd confused the translation. But a second reading told me it was so. Mariana was ill once more, and alone.

First I was angry at the disease, the murderer, and even at God. Once composed, however, I hurried to my telephone, hoping to find *someone* who knew *anyone* in Mariana's town. But I met dead ends.

I bundled books and tapes. Wondered if they'd arrive intact. Wondered if she'd understand. I kept thinking, We're blessed in America. Within minutes we can make contact with prayer partners—folks who'll pray, hug, remind us of God's love. But what about my friend Mariana?

At my kitchen table, the answer came: Hadn't He persuaded me to tuck the magazines in, prepared me even before I'd left the States? Hadn't my husband happily skied with men he barely knew, when normally he'd have made plans to include me? Hadn't I prayed for a friend, boarded a bus, and, because He's Lord of the entire globe, met Mariana in time?

This morning my friend's second letter arrived. In it I read that the tapes and books did arrive safely. She says they "mean so much to me." She remembers the sharing; it's giving her "much to think about." The articles are "very nice and convincing." And "your books you send make good reading for me." She's feeling much better, though another lump has developed, and she'll make regular visits "to control." She closes with the hope we will one day ski together and share more of "that most excellent pizza and walk in snowy woods."

Yes, I asked for a friend, and God answered that prayer. But more important is the fact that He allowed me—led me—to *become* a friend to Mariana that she might proclaim, "At last I am happy in a way unknown until now."

The Ministry of Saying No

For years I took on one "Christian duty" after another, because I feared rejection, because I feared being considered "unchristian," and because I feared being circulated through prayer chains for not conforming. With little time to bake one cake, I produced *three* from *scratch!* I detested nursery detail but volunteered anyway. In one church, I actually became responsible for potty-chairs, crackers, and juice!

Longing for approval, I surrendered outside the church too. If neighbors developed spring fever, they called me, certain I'd shelve *my* plans and gallivant. A "good Christian woman," I couldn't admit I abhorred shopping and always returned home depressed. I bought a copy of *When I Say No, I Feel Guilty* (Manual J. Smith, Ph.D.), but a friend asked to borrow it. You can guess the rest.

Occasionally I suggested I "might be unavailable" and that I performed some jobs like an elephant hides in a pint-sized jar. But refusals generated self-condemnation *and* counsel: "You're becoming disagreeable in your old age."

One day I told a pastor, "I yearn for time to write, read, and tackle *my* goals. Besides, God might not be in every 'good' thing I do 'for' Him."

My friend implied I needed prayer.

I said I needed a break!

He suggested scriptures, those warning us not to consider ourselves more highly than others.

Concluding middle-aged pollywogs stood no chance of becoming full-fledged frogs, I submitted again: decorated bulletin boards, wiped noses, led choirs, dipped dishes in bleach after fellowship meals, and vowed, "One day I'll move to Montana and *never* come out again!"

Then one morning I discovered gray hair and deep-seated pleats. If I don't reform soon, I can forget I ever had a dream of my own, I mentally declared.

"No is such a little word. But I feel that's exactly what I'm supposed to say."

"Well, Honey, it's about time!" My husband grinned.

Bolstered by Scotty's applause, I exclaimed, "I'll start today!"

My enthusiasm lived only until I considered the cliché about old dogs and new tricks and gave up.

That's when God stepped in, turning fear into faith.

"We don't have a piano player," our president lamented. "What'll *we* do?"

Her "we" sounded like "you." I fidgeted, wrestled, and mentally wandered through Yellowstone Park in search of a lodge with an unlisted address.

Yes, I played, but I had no inclination to do so. I was interested in our fellowship's success, but I had a yearning in another direction. I planned to attend each meeting but to sit at that piano *every* month?

"No way!" I nearly screeched. "I'll pray," I mumbled. I knew I was stalling; our president knew too. I ended the day in *low* gear.

The morning of the meeting, I slipped through a side door, frowned at the baby grand, glanced toward our worship leader, and met a puzzled expression on our president's face.

My need to be "forgiven" became so intense I nearly occupied the bench. But an instant caution suggested if I sat at that piano, God would make it the hottest seat in town.

"Father," I prayed, "if You *are* saying, 'Wait,' thank You. But please send a pianist *soon.*"

"Still no piano player," our secretary announced to the treasurer. Two pairs of eyes searched mine.

I recalled a sermon on the difference between filling in and fitting in. I'm not budging; if I do, we'll all miss a blessing.

Our president appealed: "Well, girls, what'll we do?"

"Let's wait," I chirped, surprising myself. "I'm *sure* God's hand-picked someone."

"Hope you're right," several chorused while I wiggled, piano fingers clenched in my lap.

Meanwhile, someone placed music on the piano rack, another arranged flowers, Kathy checked the overhead, and officers exchanged scowls.

"God," I whispered, "I believe we serve You *best* when we operate in our *strongest* gifts. But I'm about to make a poor showing rather than none at all."

Behind me I sensed rumbling. I couldn't blame them. Fifty women had arrived, everything was in place, and within 90 seconds, worship would begin.

My back pressed against the kitchen door and my heart in my throat, I doubted, hoped, wondered if giving in would be better than growing up—and then I heard the music burst forth from the main room.

As I flew toward the meeting place, our president, Ann, grabbed me and exclaimed, "Our piano player's here!"

Dottie raced by, squeezed my hand, and whispered, "Well, you were right on target again."

"No," I mumbled, shaking. "Not 'again.' The word's 'finally.'"

We're told not only that we have varying gifts but also that "*God* has arranged the parts in the body, . . . just as *he* wanted them to be" (1 Cor. 12:18, NIV, italics added). He also says we're to "try to excel in gifts that build up the church" (14:12, NIV). Scripture doesn't suggest we grind our teeth and force ourselves.

My gift doesn't show itself in the nursery; in the kitchen I'm not at my best. I don't build up the Body in a "bulletin board ministry." At the piano I don't excel. I write. And, like Paul, "I am what I am" (1 Cor. 15:10, KJV). Furthermore, I'm convinced: When I occupy *my* niche, there'll be a lot less gritting and grinding of teeth; God will be glorified; and pianos will sing.

Love One Another? In a Traffic Jam?

Yes, she was having difficulty pulling into traffic's flow from the side street to my right. But what was I to do? Wait? Let her budge in front of me?

"No way," I mumbled. "I'm already running late."

And I was. I had manuscripts to mail, groceries to buy, a dress to return, a gift to wrap. Furthermore, I needed to get home to yank wash from off the line. Storm clouds were boiling in from the west.

I won't look at her. If I do, she'll probably think I mean to let her in. Traffic was moving slowly, and there was plenty of room behind the driver in front of me, but I pressed the gas.

Within minutes I pulled up to the post office, only to discover every parking slot was filled.

I drove around the block once, twice, and again. Finally I found a space, grabbed my briefcase and purse, and dashed up the stairs to join a line two dozen bodies long!

"This is the pits," I mumbled.

I stretched my neck toward the front of the column and spotted *her!*

"Thank you," she said, nodding to the clerk who counted her change. "Next!" She grinned at the mother of twins. Then, moving toward the exit, she passed by me and smiled.

"*Really,* Father, how did she get in front of me?" I asked, grinding my teeth.

And I'm absolutely certain the Lord replied, because within seconds, I heard in my spiritual ear, "Do you really have to ask?"

Yes, Lord

For days I'd felt pent up, overwrought, less than hopeful, almost angry. "And," I moaned, "I don't have the foggiest notion why!"

Friends in my prayer group laughed, all except Kathy.

"You've got to start saying, 'Yes, Lord,'" she said. Her tone wasn't critical, but she spoke with such intensity all eyes focused on her.

"It's true," she continued. "Several years ago I had the same problem. Turned out God had something He wanted me to do, but *I* kept blocking His plan. Then one day when I was reading my Bible, He seemed to be pointing out that I was to give Him permission, every single morning, to do *whatever* He desired to do with my day, with my life."

"Like giving Him a blank check?" I asked.

"Exactly."

"But, Kathy, you know how strong-willed I can be . . . sometimes," I admitted, laughing.

"Exactly." Kathy smiled. "I think He wants to deal with that very problem."

"Problem?"

"Problem." Kathy smiled again. "It *is* a problem, and He's trying to get through to you about a change. You can count on it."

Though my friend smiled once more, I was not assured. Furthermore, not until the following morning did I even attempt to speak the words she'd suggested.

It wasn't that I didn't desire to serve God. But I'd always expected I'd somehow "know" what He wanted beforehand. But to tell Him "yes" when I had no idea what was required of me?

It took several stammerings before I finally mumbled my pledge. However, because God is patient and stands by His promise to supply even faith, the words eventually began to flow.

That first day, as I walked through routine work, I recalled how, as a seventh grade teacher, I'd realized the importance of repetition.

So, when I'd think of Kathy's advice, I'd repeatedly whisper, "Yes, Lord. Yes, Lord."

By the second day, something began to happen. From the moment my eyes opened, I found I couldn't wait to make my pledge. The pump had been primed, and the words just seemed to spill out.

In the middle of the third day, I discovered I couldn't repeat the vow without smiling as anticipation displaced hesitation. I felt God and I had formed some new alliance, had progressed to a place where we shared on a new and different level.

It took the week, but by the end of that seven days, I was yielded and ready.

Today I'm no longer striving, because I sense a guiding hand, sense I'm not alone as I reach out and attempt new feats. My work has taken on a new dimension. Seas that would not divide for nearly three years have suddenly parted. Doors have opened to me. Opportunities to share have multiplied. And, for the first time in months, I know peace. Because a friend spoke the truth in love, I have come to a place where daily I embark on an adventure. And the passwords are "Yes, Lord."

My Friend Betty—Christianity in Action

One spring day, bitter and downcast, I approached a stranger's door and found not only a friend but a lifeline.

My case brimming with beauty products, I nudged the doorbell, shifted from one foot to the other, and spotted a woman sprinting toward me: slightly plump in denims and a red-checkered shirt, hair short and windblown, eyes dancing behind horn-rimmed glasses, and a poodle at her knees. As she smiled, I wondered if I'd seen anyone quite so beautiful.

Inside, as she surveyed my catalog, I watched her radiant face, listened to her voice, and inhaled a pot roast fragrance drifting throughout the house.

As we talked, I studied her home, sensed a warmth ours didn't possess, and spotted a fish with "Jesus" on its belly. Prayers and pictures glorified Him on the entry and kitchen walls. Betty's open Bible didn't resemble ours either: hers was falling apart.

Betty's youngest, freckle-faced Christopher, darted into the room for hugs. Under his baseball cap, I caught sight of his mom's smile. Kids hopped and pushed through the house. Even the dog leaped in unrestrained anticipation. The house was happy, and Betty seemed to be the reason.

She's special, I thought, as she grinned, talked about her family, asked about mine.

I immediately moved to exit, but tears erupted.

I was shocked, and from Betty's expression, I sensed she was too. But after I'd unloaded for more than an hour, she asked if I'd come back again.

"Definitely not!" I exploded. Collecting my wits and samples, I apologized for taking her time and repeated my "no." However, as I crammed catalogs into my bag, Betty's voice became firm.

"All right. I'll come to your house then," she said.

My resistance conquered, I nodded an "OK," rushed to my car, abandoned my work, and hurried to home and seclusion.

The following day, Betty made the first of many visits. She never seemed too busy for me; she came as often as I'd allow. I'd share, weep, complain, and question, and she'd listen, read from her Bible, and pray. And when it seemed I'd discarded every anger, it was Betty's turn.

Betty was unlike Christians I'd known. Yes, I'd had Christian friends. I felt certain *I* was a Christian. I'd accepted the Lord in high school. There'd been Sunday School and camp. I sang with the adults and directed the youth. Played the piano, joined the women's group, and taught Bible school. My babies were baptized and fell asleep, nightly, to "Jesus loves you; this I know." I did know Jesus loved *them;* I just didn't know He loved *me* too. Until Betty.

Earlier when I'd shared problems with Christians, I'd received scriptures, books, and promises: "We'll pray at our next meeting." But none fully understood. When my life seemed beyond hope, complete with a divorce that climaxed years of thin commitment and unforgiveness, I withdrew.

When Betty visited, she did say she'd pray "for me," but she also prayed *with* me. She suggested scriptures to read, but she also brought a bag of Bibles and devotionals, and we read together. She even dialed a Christian station on *my* radio and ordered, "Leave it there."

Betty suggested, pleaded, chided, and argued until I bought my own Bible, a translation I finally understood. Then she suggested I attend a Bible study. When I balked, she drove me to the church and signed us *both* up!

Eventually, Betty realized I needed professional counseling, and she told me so. I said I'd see one. But she knew. On our way to lunch, she drove to a counseling center and introduced me to the staff. When I wasn't certain I could handle the fee, she even offered to pay.

Betty anticipated my every need, checked with the Lord, and often astounded me with the plans she made for us.

Near the end of my counseling, Betty said she had tickets for a luncheon with Christian women, a "special" speaker, and prayer. "And," she said, "*you're* going."

Honestly! This is absolutely the last straw, I thought. My counselor says I'm growing. Yes, there's something "small" bothering me, but I'm better! However, I soon discovered God doesn't settle for "better." It's His *best* He wants for and from us.

Midway through lunch, the speaker began talking about inner healing and being done with painful memories, and I took it all in. After weeks of prayer and preparation, I received complete release and walked away from anger—joy-filled.

For a while, we continued our weekly study together until I began teaching in a Christian school and Betty resumed her ministry to anyone God sent her way. Coveting minutes we might spare, we'd meet for lunch or coffee and talk about our delight in Him. Even when I traveled, I always knew she was there at the other end of the line, ready to share and to pray—until one year later when the Lord called her home.

Doctors had given Betty two years; God gave her five. She might have raged or completely withdrawn, but she almost never did. Instead, in pain and often hindered, she worshiped Him, studied His Word, and shared Him even in the hospital. Betty, in her quiet and unassuming way, never stopped ministering.

When she died, I understood David's grieving for his friend Jonathan. My pain, at times, became anger. I didn't understand. But because the Lord has become my Life, I found I could accept. Betty was gone from family and friends, but she'd been God's willing handmaiden. And through her, He'd revealed a great truth: Living His Word is the true manifestation of faith.

They say, "If you give a man a fish, you feed him for a day. If you teach him to fish, you feed him for life."

Betty taught me to fish.